USEFUL TECHNIQUES FOR
WOODTURNERS

The best from **WOODTURNING** magazine

USEFUL TECHNIQUES FOR
WOODTURNERS

The best from **WOODTURNING** magazine

GUILD OF MASTER CRAFTSMAN PUBLICATIONS LTD

This collection first published 1998
by Guild of Master Craftsman Publications Ltd,
Castle Place, 166 High Street, Lewes, East Sussex BN7 1XU

© GMC Publications 1998

ISBN 1 86108 078 6

Printed and bound in Hong Kong by Dai Nippon Printing Company

Front cover photograph supplied by Ron Fernie
Back cover photograph supplied by Maurice Mullins

NOTES

Please note that names, addresses, prices etc. were correct at the time the articles were originally published, but may since have changed.

CONTENTS

INTRODUCTION

Since it began, *Woodturning* has grown in stature to be the leading magazine covering the subject world-wide. Over that time the variety of techniques published has been just amazing. There seems to be no end to the ingenuity shown in the widely varied methods used and invented by woodturners.

Many woodturners work alone, so maybe this is the source of the originality of some of the techniques published in this compilation. There is no one to ask, so the 'needs must' philosophy ensues and new techniques get invented.

I have some particular favourites in this book, from the high tech RS3000 ornamental turning device in Eureka, to Geoff O'Loughlin's Poleless Pole Lathe.

I hope you enjoy the 38 articles reprinted here, and find them constructive and useful in your turning.

Terry Porter
Editor
Woodturning

BOXING CLEVER

Maurice Mullins describes how he has invented a device with which box lids can be carved and decorated

It was the late David Pye's book about woodcarving and turning that did it! In particular, his 'fluting engine' and the special lathe he used for decorating turned boxes.

The book inspired me to make my own boxes, but how to make a device on which to cut the carved and decorated lids?

The answer came a few months later, while I was swinging and adjusting my lathe's toolrest! All I'd need was a cutter, a fulcrum and a handle or lever to direct the cutter. Best of all, my own lathe toolpost would act as the fulcrum.

I quickly set about sketching a prototype, and found a piece of 300 x 20 x 5mm, 12 x ¾ x ³⁄₁₆in, flat mild-steel bar in the workshop.

Tool post

I drilled and tapped the end of the bar to give a tool post arrangement similar to that of an engineering lathe. I could therefore try out different cutters.

Next, I drilled a hole about 20mm, ¾in from one end. I tapped a hole in a piece of 32mm 1¼in diameter mild steel rod – this being the size of the inside diameter of my lathe's tool post. The lever arrangement was bolted to the top of the new post.

For the HSS cutter to fit the tool holder, I ground a piece of 6mm,¼ high speed steel bar, then fitted the complete device to my lathe.

The first trial was on the end grain of a 50mm, 2in diameter cylinder of apple wood and surprise, surprise, the device worked well! After my smug satisfaction had worn off, I found areas

A variety of box lid patterns.

▶

which could be improved upon.

First, the actual cutter was more of a scraper, and although it worked well on hard, dense woods such as lignum or box, I wanted something that would give a clean cut on a wider ranger of woods.

The next cutter was made from a 3mm,⅛in spindle gouge, bought when I didn't know any better, and not strong enough for my normal work.

I cut a piece from the gouge about 20mm, ¾in long and sharpened the cutting edge like my bowl gouge, with shoulders well back.

Slipstone

I also honed it with a slipstone, to give as clean a cut as possible and possibly longer between sharpenings.

I next discovered that by altering the distance from the cutter to the fulcrum I could alter the radii, so a different length of cut would appear.

I simply had to drill a few more holes at suitable intervals. This enabled specific radii of cut, from shallow shorts to long straighter cuts.

I now realised that by altering the height of the cutter, I could obtain a spiral effect. Until then, I'd used the toolpost as the pivot, so to adjust the height locked the tool and relied on the threaded bolt as the pivot. Demonstrating in my workshop at

Using a parting tool, separate the base from the lid.

Hollow inside the lid with a scraper and cut a rebate.

Whelpo Farm in the Lake District I discovered a part-solution which at least allowed me to raise or lower the cutter tip and use the tool post as a pivot – £1 coins.

It took two coins to raise the cutter tip to the same height as the centre height of the lathe, and another two to raise the cutter 3 to 6mm, ⅛-¼in.

Now for the difficult bit – to remove the four coins to give a cutting height of 3 or 6mm below centre.

Getting started

Close grain wood gets the best result with the jig, so I'm using apple here.

First, mount a block of wood 80 x 50 x 50mm, 3 ⅛ x 2 x 2in between centres and reduce to a cylinder. Make a spigot to fit your chuck.

Cut other spigots on both ends so that either can be designed to be the top or the bottom.

Using a parting tool, separate the base from the lid, leaving the lid firmly in the chuck.

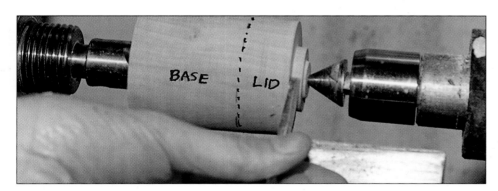

Make a spigot to fit your collet chuck on both ends of the blank.

Jig available

'The Ornamental Decorating Jig,' developed by Maurice Mullins costs £21.95 inc. VAT, from Craft Supplies Ltd, The Mill, Millers Dale, Nr Buxton, Derbyshire, SK17 8SN.
Tel: 01298 871636. Fax: 01298 872263.

Replace the lid with the base of the box and start preliminary hollowing with a gouge.

Photo 6 Cut a lip that will allow the lid to fit firmly on the base.

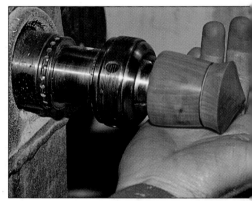

Photo 7 Shalping, sanding and polishing completed.

Hollow out inside lid with a scraper. Cut your rebate, then finish in your chosen way. I use sunflower oil, which makes fitting the lid to the base quite slippery, so I gently re-cut the rebate to remove any traces of oil that could have strayed onto the friction fit surfaces.

Base of the box

Remove the lid from the chuck and replace with the base of the box.

I cut a good size rebate to allow the lid a firm fit between lid and base. It needs to be a firm fit, as the lever tool generates a lot of side force during the cut. If a lid is too tight, tap it sharply on the underside to remove, with the edge of a 12mm, ½in scraper.

▶

After sanding and polishing, Maurice sets up his lever tool in the lathe's toolpost. Coins are used to adjust cutter height.

Jam the lid on the base and shape the outside to more or less your final design. Either sand and finish the outside of the box or leave it to be finished last.

Before I deal with the inside of the base, I set up my lever tool in the lathe's toolpost.

Same shape

I roughly shape the lid to the same shape the cutter describes in its radial cut. This lessens the possibility of the cutter taking too big a cut – possibly pushing the lid off!

You can use a dividing head to give regular formalised patterns, but I like to judge the spacing by hand. Practise setting up the cutter and manually judging the spacing. When actually

Timbers

Amerillo
(*Centrolobium sp.*)

Apple
(*Malus sp.*)

Boxwood, European
(*Buxus sempervirens*)

Holly
(*Ilex sp.*)

Lignum Vitae
(*Guaiacum sp.*)

Sycamore
(*Acer pseudoplatanus*)

doing the decorative cuts, keep saying to yourself, "Cut-Back-Rotate, Cut-Back-Rotate." This order of operation is important.

If you don't bring the cutter back along the path it has just cut, it will be forced back over the uncut wood, and this is likely to push the tool out of alignment.

The photo below (left) shows positioning of the tool post so the cutter is starting its cut about 2mm, ³⁄₃₂in in from the edge and travelling to its finish about 1mm, ³⁄₆₄in from the lid's apex.

When setting up I sometimes revert to what I call a 'vernier' adjustment in the form of a copper-headed mallet – to gently persuade the cross slide into the correct position before clamping down fully.

I must stress the importance of practise. Don't expect to make a gallery-type bowl or box inside 10 minutes!

Box-making practise will give you the confidence in your abilities to cut a tight-fitting lid, which is essential in this project. ∎

Four versions of the lever tool (left to right): Maurice Mullins's prototype; his prototype with modified tool holder; a version now made by Craft Supplies, who also sell most of the necessary tool post attachments to fit your lathe; and another improvement, made for Maurice by Gordon Fradley, of the Mid-Staffs group.

Positioning the toolpost with cutter at centre height.

A close-up of the lever tool's cutting action.

Box of cutters with handle and extension sockets.

Cecil Jordan is an independent craftsman working in a variety of materials. He has a sponsor's mark as a goldsmith but is chiefly known for his work as a professional turner. A former pupil of Douglas Hart, his work has been bought by the V and A for the National Collection, by South West Arts, Southern Arts, the Crafts Council and numerous other public and private collections. He is represented on the index of Craftsmen maintained by the Crafts Council and is a regular exhibitor at Contemporary Applied Arts. He is an Assessor for the Register of Professional Turners of the Worshipful Company of Turners and a visiting tutor at West Dean and Parnham. He gives summer school courses for the latter.

Cecil's interest in ornamental turnery stems from the work done on an Evans ornamental lathe by a distant relative. He now is the possessor of this lathe. Pieces made on the machine have been presented to members of the Royal Family by the Worshipful Company of Turners — four pieces which won the Company's Gold Medal in 1924 to the Queen Mother on the occasion of her marriage and a rattle to Princess Beatrice in 1988 when she was christened.

RESTORING & SHARPENING OT CUTTING TOOLS

CECIL JORDAN

When Cecil Jordan acquired a set of old OT cutters they were so badly rusted he almost threw them away. But he decided instead to restore them to usable condition. This is how he did it.

Within the past year an odd batch of cutters for an ornamental turner's lathe came into my possession. The condition was so poor that I was on the point of throwing them all away. The problem was that they were pitted with rust on the top face and had been incorrectly sharpened. By that I mean the top faces were no longer flat along their length but bevelled off towards the cutting edge — an evil of unparalleled magnitude in my workshop.

However, ornamental cutters are ornamental cutters when all is said and done, made with great precision by craftsmen whose skills I envy, and not lightly to be discarded.

Let's start at the beginning. Lathes for ornamental turning were made with the main purpose of turning ivory, a material of great beauty and great price. Anything made from another material was regarded, generally speaking, as a practice piece.

Raw ivory cut across the grain and left in unsuitable conditions would develop radial cracking similar to that which appears on the end of a seasoning log. So there are tensions in it. Tensions maybe, but there is no actual 'grain' or what you might call 'fibre'. The whole is a cohesive mass and turns equally well at any angle to the directions of growth, almost like metal or a man-made material. We will touch upon these again in a moment.

The woodturner who uses his tools correctly is striving at every opportunity to induce his hand-held tool to cut in such a mode that the bevel of his tool is rubbing on the surface just prepared by the cutting edge. It comes as a shock, and a severe one at that, to realise that if he starts ornamental turning the mode of removing material is what he regards as scraping. And he knows that this won't do.

Well, actually, it will do, because of two factors in particular. One is the angle of

Handle and extension sockets for ornamental cutters.

approach of the tool, either fixed or revolving, and the other is the way in which the cutting tool is sharpened. The attention to detail of the bevel and the quality of finish of the facet or facets is a completely different standard to woodturning tools. So much so that it will work quite well even on wood.

There are several sizes and patterns of these cutters and they may be divided basically according to the ways in which they are held:

Slide rest tools, the largest. They are used in a fixed position and, on occasion, have to bear a good deal of battering. Included in this group are chasers for cutting threads.

Tools for the vertical cutting frame which has a

'The top faces were no longer flat along their length but bevelled off towards the cutting edge — an evil of unparalleled magnitude in my workshop.'

vertical, circular motion.

Tools for the horizontal cutting frame which has a horizontal, circular motion.

Tools for the universal cutting frame which can be adjusted to cut at any angle between vertical and horizontal.

Tools for these last three cutting frames are of precisely the same section as the sliderest tools but they are much shorter, only about a quarter of the length.

Tools for the eccentric cutting frame which cuts eccentric circles of varying diameters. These are the smallest of the cutting frame tools.

The drill. This revolves concentrically and the tools have round shanks, not

rectangular like the others. All may be fitted into a handle so that they can be hand held and all may be fitted into extension sockets for sharpening if required.

We will now look at the factors which need to be considered when sharpening these tools.

It has to be said that almost every material handled on the lathe of the ornamental turner, other than ivory, will produce a finish that is a compromise. This includes wood in particular and also man-made materials which, for our convenience,

may be grouped under the heading of plastics. I have turned most of the currently available man-made materials and have found none which is really satisfactory on all counts.

So we are going to scrape wood, and scrape it to such effect that the finish has to be that left by the tool — no sanding or polishing other than with a small, stiffish brush will be possible. The lustrous finish associated with the best ornamental turning is dependent mainly upon the cutting edge of the tool.

Back, then, to the dispiriting collection of ironmongery. The first approach was to remove as much of the rust as possible to appraise the extent of the problem. This can be done using either one of two liquid preparations readily obtainable to everyone. There may be others.

Paraffin and oil used in the ratio 4:1. Soak objects for 24 hours and then examine them. This may be long enough. Give them a stir occasionally, brush with a stiff brush, wash with detergent and then water.

Vinegar and salt used in the ratio 1 quart: 2 tablespoons. Soak for up to three days agitating the objects from time to time, then wash with water.

I chose the second recipe using a lidded, plastic box. The smell is terrible. After washing and drying it was clear that there was a significant problem with these cutters — surface rust pits. Again they were almost discarded as the thought of the number of hours of rubbing down was unbearable.

There was however another, and drastic, possible treatment, to take all the top surfaces off by horizontal grinding. This

means holding the cutters down by magnetism and grinding the top surfaces off at the rate of half a thou, at a pass. Some grinders produce a lovely finish, some do not.

But there is something else. Most cutters of whatever size have a number stamped on the top surface. These numbers may denote the facial angles in profile or the width of the cutting edge in hundredths of an inch.

By the look of the rust pits, removal of these would also remove the numbers. Removal of the illegal bevel would do the same. Would this number removal be regarded as a criminal act? Well, it was that or discard the tools so the decision was made to go ahead.

Few turners possess hori- ▶

zontal grinding machines with electro-magnetic beds so help had to be sought and was eventually found at a reasonable price, but not a very good result because the grinding wheel was too coarse.

Well now, despite the desirability of little cabinets with drawers full of tools the fact is that, in its early stages at any rate, ornamental turning can be done with very few cutters. As few as three shapes will give a wide range of possibilities:

1) A full round using the total width of the cutter for all cutting frames and the sliderest.

2) An included angle of 120 DEG ground to a central point for all cutting frames and the sliderest.

3) A fine, round shape using a tapering point for the sliderest only.

So we are looking at seven cutters as a start. Things now begin to look a little more reasonable. Never mind the numbers, I am beginning to say to myself, use your common sense.

The rubbing down of surfaces by hand after grinding is known as lapping and that is what we are now about. There are various options, diamond-impregnated surfaces, oil-stones, wet and dry papers on glass under water and Japanese water stones.

Oilstones quite quickly wear into hollows and have to be trued up themselves. Wet and dry papers will always inevitably form a little wave ahead of the tool and round off the front end, and Japanese water stones are very soft, although they can easily be trued up. More of these in a moment.

We are left with diamonds, which are just about to become someone's 'best friend'.

There are three types of abrasive applications using diamonds in the solid state which are currently readily available:

Ceramic tiles, reputedly a

spin-off from the space programme. They are very hard and are used with an aerosol-applied diamond slurry. The same objection is raised as with papers, a little wave builds up in front of the cutter and rounds off the end. Also the aerosol liquid evaporates too quickly leaving a surface with too much friction.

Tiles with islands of diamonds embedded in the surface. These are not as effective as:

6mm ¼″ steel plates with diamonds embedded throughout. This last option is the best that I have found yet. It stays absolutely flat for years and years. Mine is years old and is still just as flat as ever. It is used dry, comes in fine grade only and is made in America. It is available in the UK from a firm called Tilgear.

We are now into lapping to achieve the perfect flat top surface to our cutter. Nothing less than perfection will do but once done it will never have to be done again so stick with it.

Next is the bevel. Both Evans and Holtzapffel agree, as well they might, that an angle off vertical of 30-35 DEG is the optimum angle for hardwoods and to achieve this requires a hand-held sharpening jig for preference. There are two considerations here, the angle of the bevel and the angle of the profile. The device used for holding the cutter for this sharpening operation is known as a goniostat.

Jig for sharpening ornamental cutters which have convex cutting edges.

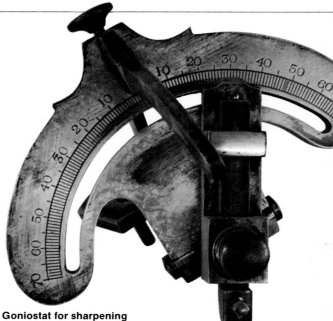

Goniostat for sharpening ornamental cutters which have plane facets and straight angles.

I was introduced to the hand-sharpening of tools at the age of 11 and although I haven't done it every day since I have done it most weeks and sometimes several times a day for some weeks together. Despite this I would not attempt what I have seen recommended by some writers — the hand sharpening of ornamental cutters.

I have only to take a cursory look at the proper thing to realise that I cannot, and never will, manage those crisp angles and perfect facets by hand. You have to examine all these ground surfaces with a x 10 magnifying glass — ordinary eyesight, however good, is not nearly good enough.

So a goniostat you have to have. You may have to make your own or you may be able to buy one at auction, but have one you must.

Goniostats stand on three legs. The two back ones are part of the jig and the third, the front one, is the tool to be ground. It is held in place by a thumbscrew and adjusted for angles laterally and vertically. The two rear legs move on a lubricated glass plate and the front one rubs on the diamond plate — they must be the same height.

When the facet of one of the cutting angles is finished, exchange the diamond plate for the finest grade. Japanese water stone that you can obtain. A surprisingly few passes will produce a mirror-like finish which suddenly makes you realise what the whole thing is about — use your magnifying glass.

Now do the other facet and admire. There will be a burr on the top edge of the facets. Remove it by rubbing the top surface on the diamond plate once more but make sure to keep it flat.

The Japanese water stone will wear very quickly because it is soft. To true it up use a shallow plastic tray of the type used for cat litter and a 6mm ¼″ thick sheet of glass with rounded corners and edges. Fix a sheet of 150 grit wet and dry to the glass using double-sided tape or aerosol fixative. Immerse the glass sheet in water in the tray and carefully rub the water stone on the abrasive sheet. It will soon be restored to flatness.

By doing all this we have created another evil. The thickness of the cutter is now less than it is supposed to be and this matters on two counts. One, the cutter may slide in the cutting frame or sliderest and will therefore need packing with a little piece of shim. And two, the height of centre of the tool will have to be checked meticulously every time the tool is changed, which should be done anyway.

The sharpening of cutting tools which have curved profiles requires a different technique. Convex cutters can be attended to using a jig which complements the goniostat. It has only two feet, one is a ball carried on a rod and the other is the cutter itself (see the photograph). Check the angle of the bevel before using.

Bead drills and moulding drills with concave cutting edges require the use of a revolving cone carrying an abrasive paste. These cones can be made of brass formed on the lathe using high speed steel tools. They properly have grooves running their length to retain the paste. This paste used to be oilstone powder with oil. Valve grinding paste is the current alternative or diamond slurry with vaseline.

The concave cutter is passed up to the cone until it fits the diameter, making sure abrasion takes place equally on each side of the curve. Reversing the direction of the cone helps in this respect and reminds you of the advantage of a treadle. A slow speed helps here. These little tools demand concentration and skill. In some cases slip stones or diamond impregnated files are a help. Try Tilgear again for files.

This attention to detail is essential to avoid the cause of dull reflections from cut surfaces. Unless the cutting edges of these tools are free from blemishes they will produce lines or striations on the finished surfaces and reflections will be broken. On wood it is useless to expect good results without a mirror finish at the bevel and top surface of the tool. Both Evans and Holtzapffel suggest a microbevel to give the best results possible.

It may pass through the mind of the 'lapper' that there are

'Many of my cutters are likely to be 100 years old or more. I feel I owe it to past and future generations to see that these delightful objects are around in another 100 years.'

other ways of handling these matters — for example if the metal were to be annealed then flatting would be easier. However, hardening after flattening, if not carried out perfectly evenly, can create distortion and the re-numbering of cutters can also distort if hit with the necessary force.

Some of the problems with rusty cutters may be caused by keeping them in cabinets. It may be because of the close-fitting rectangular slots in which the cutters stand. If the wood

the cutters do tend to face in different directions.

I am aware, however, that many, if not all of my cutters are likely to be 100 years old or more. I feel I owe it to past as well as future generations to see that these delightful objects are around in another 100 years.

At this point you might well be asking "What about other kinds of cutting tools?" Well, some eccentric cutting frame tools have been tipped with a correctly angled and polished

available with a cutting frame devised by Paul Fletcher. They are made from 1/8 round section material and have to be sharpened with diamond-impregnated wheels or plates. This cutting frame was originally intended for use with a rose engine lathe but is suitable for ornamental turning of a less esoteric nature.

Useful addresses: For further information concerning this cutting frame, and other matters concerning ornamental turning, contact the Secretary to the Society of Ornamental Turners: Nicholas Edwards, 188 Bromham Road, Bedford, Beds. MK40 4BP.

Supplier: Tilgear, Bridge House, 69 Station Road, Cuffley, Herts. EN6 4TG. Tel: 01707 873434.

Goniostat and another jig for sharpening ornamental cutters showing brass plate, oil stone and iron plate on which cutters used to be sharpened. Also a few of the types of ornamental cutters showing numbers and, in some cases, the maker's name, Fenn.

absorbs moisture and then sweats with the attendant acids and tannins coming into solution then the cutters can seize up in the slots. I prefer circular slots which give greater air circulation, although they perhaps don't look so nice and

diamond. It will not need sharpening but is prone to shattering if dropped or incorrectly applied. The cost is such that currently about 50 Holtzapffel or Evans cutters in a box can be bought at auction for the same price.

Then there is high-speed steel. Given the availability of material of the right dimensions this would certainly hold a cutting edge longer. I would not know where to obtain a supply.

Solid tungsten cutters are

This article refers to the volumes by Holtzapffel, and readers will recall that we reviewed the reprinted paperback Volumes 4 and 5 of this important work in Issue 6 of *Woodturning*. Volume 5 deals with the sharpening of tools, and the use of the goniostat is also discussed at length in Volume 3. Unless you are fortunate enough to possess a complete set of Holtzapffel, you will have difficulty referring to Volume 3 as it has been out of print for many years. However, Cecil Jordan's approach to the problem is a much updated solution — Ed. ■

Allan Beecham's Skewchigouge and an example of its work. The tool has a slightly concave 'flat' and a rounded 'bevel' like a gouge.

Allan Beecham, inventor of the distinctively named Skewchigouge, tells how both the tool – and the name – came about

The Skewchigouge (pronounced Skoo-cheegouge) is easier to use than it is to say. It's a tool which does everything the skew can do – in some cases more – but in greater safety.

The tool's genesis goes back about 25 years, when Peter Chapman, a fine turner who is also my brother-in-law, showed me a gouge he used. This was a strange-looking beast, with a long tip and the wings ground back on both sides. It enabled him to do all cuts – including those usually made with a skew chisel.

I was so impressed I decided to make my own. I tried it out on wood as hard as nails, which a customer had supplied. But the tip kept breaking and I was on the grindstone more than the lathe. I persevered for a time, because the tool never kicked back (or caught a crab as we we say in the East End, where I grew up). Eventually, I put it aside, trying again periodically, with the same result – broken tips.

Then, one day last year, I tried a slightly different grind on it. The thought came to me that perhaps the reason for the tip snapping was that there was no support for it. What would be the result if I used a straight bar and ground that in precisely the same way?

I tried it and bingo, it worked a treat. And so the tool was born. But what to call it? A 'sisel' did not have the right ring. What about a Skewchiselgouge. A bit too long. I had it – the Skewchigouge!

What's in a name

The gouge works wonderfully well in some areas, especially in turning half hollows (my old word for a 'cove', which I find ugly), hollows with a bead in the bottom, or balls with a bead on top. ➤

Half hollow　　　　**Hollow with bead**　　　　**Ball with bead**

In this view of the Skewchigouge, the rounded 'bevel' is uppermost.

► These jobs can be done easily with this tool, which shifts from being a gouge to a chisel and back again, making life for the amateur woodturner a pleasure.

One customer described the Skewchigouge as 'user-friendly,' and told me it had given him the confidence to return to the skew.

In use

When re-grinding or sharpening the Skewchigouge, ensure that the top surface, looking straight on, is not pointed (fig 1), but rounded (fig 2). Also make sure that the face,

when looked at sideways on, is not shaped flat (fig 3) but concave (fig 4).

After roughing to a round, I use a 'rubbing the bevel' technique. This means the tool should be placed on the rest first and the bevel rubbed on the revolving wood. The handle is brought up slowly, until the gouge starts to cut. When this happens, the tool should be moved forward in the direction of the cut, cutting and rubbing at the same time.

I can't guarantee it, but I hope the Skewchigouge solves at least some of your turning problems. Good luck! ■

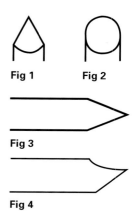

Fig 1   Fig 2

Fig 3

Fig 4

How to use the Skewchigouge

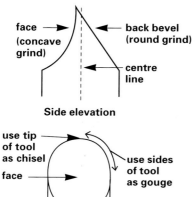

face → (concave grind)

← back bevel (round grind)

← centre line

Side elevation

use tip of tool as chisel

face →

→ use sides of tool as gouge

Front elevation

Chopping in must be done in chisel mode with the tip of the tool

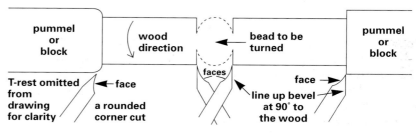

pummel or block

wood direction

bead to be turned

pummel or block

T-rest omitted from drawing for clarity

← face

a rounded corner cut

faces

face →

line up bevel at 90° to the wood

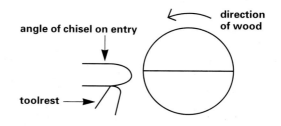

angle of chisel on entry

direction of wood

toolrest →

Allan Beecham comes from generations of woodworkers and turners. He began turning at the age of 13, learning his skills from his father, Sidney Albert Beecham.

He started work when he was 15, drilling holes in lamps with his father. Later, he was employed by a number of firms in London's East End. Over 30 years ago, Allan, his father and three brothers started a turning business.

He worked there until about 17 years ago, when he branched out on his own and set up Calamus Woodturning, first at Horam and then Burwash, in East Sussex.

Turn with the Skewchigouge

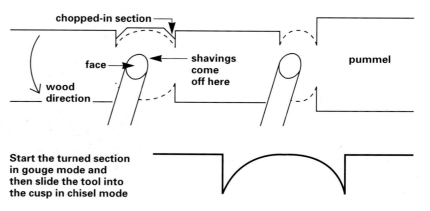

chopped-in section

face →

← shavings come off here

wood direction

pummel

Start the turned section in gouge mode and then slide the tool into the cusp in chisel mode

PAPER WORK

Ken Sager explains how he uses paper joints in his turning

Ernie Conover wrote about using paper joints in turning some time ago (*Woodturning* Issue 13). I have developed the technique to suit my own work.

Paper joints are an old way of attaching a sacrificial piece of waste wood to a workpiece. A piece of paper is glued between the waste and the work, so screws, clamps and vices used to hold the waste don't damage the work.

On completion, a sharp blade is used to split the paper, leaving the easy job of scraping glue and paper from the workpiece.

For eight years I have used paper joints to hold most of my turnings and have developed a few tricks. The paper I use is a 70g/m² white printing paper. I buy the ends of rolls from a local printing works for a few New Zealand dollars. It's also good for drawing designs on.

Less strain

If the turning is thin, about 3mm, ⅛", I use craft card which separates more easily than paper. Less strain is put on the work, so there is less chance of breaking it.

The adhesive I use is a five minute epoxy resin from Bostik. It is extremely strong, quick setting and easily cleaned off the work by power sanding.

It comes in two parts, resin and hardener, and it's a good idea to hinge the lids on the tins with strips of sticky tape. This avoids mixing up the lids, which would permanently glue them on. I also use separate sticks to dip resin and hardener from the tins.

All my work is mounted on a backing board, which is then screwed on to a 150mm, 6" faceplate. The backing board is not necessarily round. On larger work it's about 300mm, 12" wide, and the length is about three-quarters the diameter of the work.

The speeds I turn at are 250 RPM for

work up to about 610mm, 24" and 150 RPM for larger work, up to 1220mm, 48".

First, the blank is mounted straight on the faceplate and the outside turned. I turn a foot on the bottom, to help with centralising, and give it a wide flat rim for the joint.

With the outside and foot turned I mount the backing board on the faceplate and cut a 3mm, ⅛" recess in it for the foot. The foot should neatly fit the recess to centralised the remounted bowl. The bottom of the recess must be flat, to make a good surface for gluing.

Bead of epoxy

Cut the paper to fit inside the recess and glue it in with a bead of epoxy. Do not get adhesive on the side of the recess, or you will have trouble separating the joint.

The bowl is glued to the paper with another bead of epoxy, and clamped or weighted as the glue dries.

I sometimes support the bowl with wedges cut to the shape of the outside and glued on with more paper joints.

When the inside of the bowl is completed, I first break the paper joints on the corner blocks with a broad, sharp chisel. I then use a tyre lever to break the main paper joint.

If the finish on the outside is good, adhesive won't penetrate and patches can be peeled off, especially if the wood is oily. Otherwise it can be pared off with the chisel then sanded.

I have used this system on bowls up to 1525mm, 60" DIA, and ones as deep as 457mm, 18", and I haven't had a joint fail yet. ■

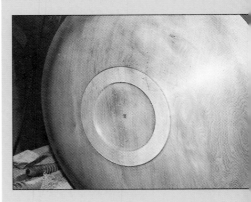

The outside is turned on a faceplate and finished, having a foot with a wide flat rim.

The recess turned in the backing board, a bead of epoxy adhesive ready for the paper.

When the bowl is finished the paper joints are broken, first at the support blocks then on the backing board.

The completed bowl ready for rim embellishment.

RAY LEVY

Toolmaker Ray Levy has adapted an old machine shop technique for ornamental turning, which allows him to use materials previously thought unsuitable for this exacting, time-consuming craft.

ZEST FOR ZIGZAGS

Zigzag-patterned after early native American pottery designs, these bowls present a different approach to ornamental turning, as they're made from hardwoods previously considered unsuitable for ornamental turnery.

For bowl blanks cut from plank it is only necessary the wood be fine-textured, and sufficiently strong that the points won't break off the teeth where they have short grain crossing them.

If the long grain is vertically oriented in the bowl there will be no short grain crossings and many more woods become useable.

It is advisable to test scrap pieces of various materials by cutting several teeth to sharp points directly across the grain. If no chipping occurs the wood is safe to use.

The table on page 14 shows hardwoods I have tested and rated for suitability for this work.

At first glance the geometry of such a zigzag pattern may seem simple, but it isn't. Consider a radial array of vee cuts on a flat surface, all intersecting at a common centre.

Each vee will be deepest at its outer edge, diminishing to zero at the centre, as the converging cuts reduce the heights of the teeth.

As the bottoms of the cuts are level, the tops of the teeth must slant inward. Two such similar pieces will mate only at their outer edges.

To achieve a proper fit it will be necessary to make the vee cuts on the theoretical surface of a shallow cone.

If properly done, the outward slope of the bottoms of the cuts will equal the inward slope of the tops of the teeth, so that when one part is inverted it will be a perfect fit on the other.

While you could make a large scale layout to determine the proper cone angle, it is easier to use the equation shown. This is the calculation used for angular-toothed machine clutches which are identical in design to the bowl pieces. Solving the equation gives the cross-slide angle setting for cutting the teeth.

To design such a bowl I make a full-scale layout of both inside and outside profiles and draw the decorative patterns in place. From this I can determine the inner and outer diameters of the annulus on which each pattern will be cut.

The major diameter of the blank is then multiplied by 3.14 to obtain its circumference and this is divided by the desired number of teeth giving the required cutter width.

If this width of cut exceeds that of your cutter you must try the next larger number of teeth available from your indexing system.

To begin, the blank for the base of the bowl is securely mounted to a chuck or faceplate. It must remain on this mounting through several cycles of removal and reassembly on the lathe spindle.

The blank is turned to a cylinder as measured from the layout and is recessed to leave a standing rim a little deeper than the teeth will be cut.

It's advisable to leave extra material on the inside of the rim to absorb the inevitable chipping as the cutter breaks through. An angular shoulder will reduce this chipping.

The slide rest is accurately set to the calculated angle. I use a machinist's combination

Raymond Levy received his formal woodwork training at aircraft mechanics' school. He was serving an apprenticeship as a toolmaker when World War II intervened and he found himself in the upper turret of a B-24 Liberator.

After leaving the USAF he worked for some years in the tool and die shops, eventually being recruited into the fledgeling aerospace industry.

Having operated apparatus-building shops for two different firms, he transferred to the drawing board and spent the next 20 years designing scientific apparatus.

Since retirement he has had a workshop, where he builds a variety of small, precise woodwork such as jewellery boxes, three-dimensional puzzles and wooden demonstration mechanisms. Ray is the author of *Making Mechanical Marvels in Wood* (Sterling Pub. Co. Inc.).

Ray Levy,
The Craftworks,
PO Box 804, Soquel,
CA 95073, USA.

square protractor with its base against the face of a chuck and its blade against the edge of the slide rest.

Do not turn the face of the blank to a cone, for it will increase the tooth cutting effort, as a deeper cut will be needed to bring the outer edges of the teeth to sharp points.

The horizontal cutting head is set up with the vee cutter in place. The point of the cutter

Photo 1 Base piece recessed, ready to cut teeth.

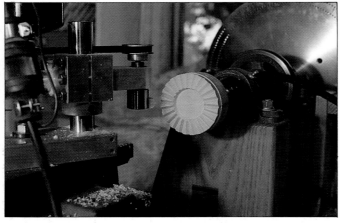

must be aligned to the spindle centreline as accurately as is possible if the parts are to fit. Any error in vertical centring will be doubled in the assembly.

The index plate is set up and adjusted for the desired number of divisions (Photo 1). The first cut is made as nearly as possible in line with the grain. I make a preliminary stack of all the blanks and mark a line on each where I want them to align at assembly.

The cutter is then aligned with this line on every other

'At first glance the geometry of such a zigzag pattern may seem simple, but it isn't. Consider a radial array of vee cuts on a flat surface, all intersecting at a common centre.'

blank, and half-a-tooth-width away on the intermediate blanks.

The first cuts can be fairly deep, about 2mm ³⁄₃₂″ (Photo 2), subsequent cuts becoming progressively wider must be of lesser depth. When the tops of the teeth have been reduced to sharp edges, I sharpen and polish the cutter, carefully reset it and take a final pass of .05mm all around.

Any splintering is now removed from the inner diameter, the teeth brushed clean and the work in its chuck removed from the lathe and sealed in a plastic bag.

The blank for the zigzag

**Photo 2
The first cut
completed.**

pattern is set up and cut exactly as before, except that the first cut is taken half-a-tooth-width from the line (Photo 3).

**Photo 3
All teeth
cut to depth
in a bubinga
piece.**

This allows a tooth from the first piece to enter the cut in this piece so the alignment marks on the blanks will coincide. If all this is a little confusing don't worry, it took me a while to work it out.

When the second part is completed, it is cleaned and removed from the lathe (Photo 4). Glue is poured into a

Photo 4 Parts ready to be glued.

Photo 5 Gluing up.

shallow dish and with a small clean brush a uniform thin coat is applied to all tooth surfaces.

The parts are immediately assembled and clamped with at least four clamps used across the work and the back side of the chuck or faceplate (Photo 5).

HOW THEY RATE

Woods tested and their ratings — 100 DEG included angle cutter

1 — Major chipping, unsatisfactory.
2 — Minor chipping visible with unaided vision.
3 — Chipping visible with 2X magnification.
4 — Chipping visible with 10X magnification.
5 — No chipping visible with 10X magnification.

Wood	Rating
Lignum vitae	5
Pernambuco	5
Orange tree	4
Mahogany	4
Padauk (African)	4
Apple	4
Cherry	3
Ceylon satinwood	3
Katalox	3
Cocobolo	3
Boxwood	3
Angelique	2
Osage orange	2
Hard maple	2
Yellow satinwood	2
Gaboon ebony	2
Bubinga	2
Almond	1
Quila	1
Rosewood	1
Peach	1

Photo 6 Trepanning the centre disc.

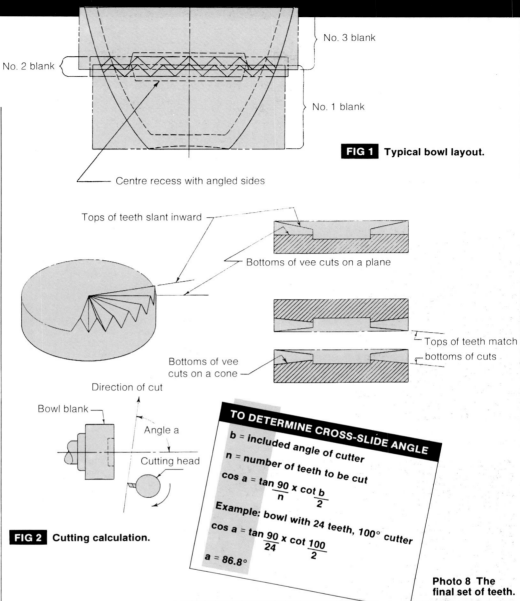

No. 2 blank

No. 3 blank

No. 1 blank

Centre recess with angled sides

FIG 1 Typical bowl layout.

Tops of teeth slant inward

Bottoms of vee cuts on a plane

Tops of teeth match bottoms of cuts

Bottoms of vee cuts on a cone

Direction of cut

Bowl blank

Angle a

Cutting head

FIG 2 Cutting calculation.

TO DETERMINE CROSS-SLIDE ANGLE

b = included angle of cutter

n = number of teeth to be cut

$$\cos a = \tan \frac{90}{n} \times \cot \frac{b}{2}$$

Example: bowl with 24 teeth, 100° cutter

$$\cos a = \tan \frac{90}{24} \times \cot \frac{100}{2}$$

$$a = 86.8°$$

Photo 8 The final set of teeth.

After drying overnight, the clamps are removed, the work remounted in the lathe and a thin-bladed tool is used to trepan the central disc out of the second piece (Photo 6).

Among other desirable features, this is an economical way of making bowls, the small bowl shown here having been made from the centre of the larger one.

The blank is now machined to near finished height and the second sequence of cuts taken to produce the zigzag pattern. To obtain a line of uniform thickness the point of the tool must be aligned with the point of the tooth below.

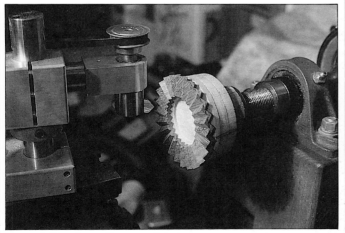

Photo 7 The zigzag line completed.

This is corrected, if necessary, by use of the adjustable index. The teeth are cut to depth as on the first two surfaces, the cuts progressing until the desired line thickness is achieved (Photo 7).

The assembly is once more unscrewed from the spindle and sealed in its plastic bag.

The last layer is cut exactly like the others (Photo 8) and glued in place. When dry the ▶

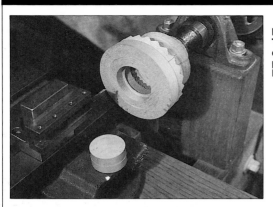

Photo 9
The removed
centre
plug can still
be used.

central disc is trepanned out (Photo 9).

I allow the completed assembly to rest for a few days to stabilise, then mount it in the lathe and turn it to shape. Cardboard templates are used for both inner and outer profiles as there isn't much room for artistic licence on a blank such as this.

The outside is turned to size and to fit the template and the inside completed (Photo 10).

I must confess to turning the entire bowl with scraping tools, having too much invested in the

completes the job (Photo 11).

Many patterns are possible using these methods. I have only begun to explore the possibilities. If you undertake such a project, I suggest you make your work station comfortable, preferably with a stool of proper height, as you will be there for some time.

My large bowl with the two rows of zigzags took more than 25 hours to complete and required 1,872 traverses of the cutting head. As Bill Jones so aptly says, 'ornamental turning is not for the impatient'. ∎

Mother and Child.

Photo 10 Ready for the finish.

blank to take any unnecessary risks.

The inside and outside of the bowl are sanded through 400 grit and four coats of a tung-oil varnish applied with the work turning. It is steel-woolled between coats.

When dry, the mounting block is parted off and the bowl held in my home-made ring chuck to turn and finish the base. (See Issue 23 for how to make this.) A coat of wax

Zigzag bowls in yellow satinwood and bubinga, 88mm 3⅜" DIA x 55mm 2⅛" H.

Photo 11 The bowl in my ring chuck, with the bottom turned, marked and finished.

Getting down to scratch

Appropriate wear for sanding, a respirator with a safety visor.

To hand sand, or power sand, that is the question. It's one wood-turners have asked themselves for many years. Bob and Ann Phillips try to answer it here and tell of a new method of sanding at very high speeds.

Sanding can be a bit of a taboo topic. For woodturners are often coy to reveal how much they use abrasives. This does nothing to help the beginner, who should remember (whatever has been hinted to the contrary) that all turners sand.

Many questions we are asked at workshops are about problems connected with finishing work. Some solve themselves in time, through improved tool control, which comes from practise, but sanding techniques are important too.

We'll describe here how you can eliminate much of the donkey work associated with sanding.

Choosing abrasives

Choosing a good abrasive is vital. The early garnet or glass papers are now used less, as woodturners find more sophisticated abrasives at their disposal.

Over the years we've used many of those marketed and have found that you really do get what you pay for, as the more expensive abrasives usually make up for their higher price in long life and efficiency.

Silicon carbide (Si C), the classic 'wet and dry' paper, and aluminium oxide (Al O) are the two main groups of papers used by woodturners. The main difference between them is in the profile of the abrasive particle of each.

The authors

Bob and Ann Phillips threw in good jobs nearly 10 years ago to become professional woodturners and have never looked back.
They supply shops and galleries throughout New Zealand and some of their pieces are in overseas collections. The couple have written a book on making money from woodturning, published by GMC Publications last year, and also wrote a three-part series for *Woodturning* on how to *Pump up the Profits*.

Hand sanding with a felt pad under the abrasive paper

Power sanding discs. The air powered sander on the left is fitted with a 'roloc' disc.

The 'roloc' abrasive disc clips into the backing pad for quick changes.

Si C is a sharp vee-shaped cutting particle, while Al O has a more shallow cutting U-shaped profile. In practice, this means the former is very sharp, but that the hard, narrow cutting edge is quickly lost. The latter is not as sharp, but is tougher, keeping its cutting edge longer.

Modern specialist papers are usually variants of these two, such as zinc stearate papers. This compound is in fact a release coating or 'dry lubricant' rather than an abrasive. It works by carrying away the 'gunk', resisting clogging as you sand.

You will see this type of paper changes colour in use, as the top coat-

FIG 1 Construction of sanding pad for power sanding.

Vinyl (Attached with contact adhesive)

10mm ⅜"

Sign board (hardboard)

Tightening nut

Lock nut

We leave a hole in the centre in case the bolt needs to be re-tightened

150mm 6"

Bolt

Soft foam rubber

Chuck

50mm 2"

Adhesive sanding discs can be fixed directly to the vinyl, or glue Velcro to the vinyl to use the Velcro-backed sanding disc

Contact adhesive joint

ing is lost. The true abrasive material (Si C or Al O) is the layer beneath this release coating.

When you sand with oil or water as lubricants these act as the release agent, carrying away the swarf in the same way as the special coatings.

Use of abrasives

You can sand either by hand with abrasive papers or by power, using abrasives held by an electric drill, angle grinder or air sanders.

The table at the end of this article gives comparative speeds for each method. These speeds are dependent on the equipment, and can vary considerably. Whether sanding by hand or power, use a light touch to keep the abrasive moving across the work.

Sanding sequence

Normally, we start at 100 or 120 grit and progress to finer ones to achieve the desired surface finish. Each one should remove the scratches left by the former. A suitable sequence would be 120, 180, 220, and 400, though for some work you may go on to use 600 or 1200.

With some woods, a few coarser grits may be needed, so the sequence could start with an 80 or even 60 grit.

As all sanding involves risk from fine particles of wood and from fragments of the abrasive, it's essential you protect yourself with close fitting visors and respirator masks.

Ensure the basic safety requirements are met, no matter how quick the sanding operation. For example, the toolrest should be angled or taken off the lathe, so it can't make painful contact with your hand.

A soft pad

Use a soft pad to support the sanding paper or cloth, perhaps foam or thick felt. If, as turners sometimes prefer, you use a wad of wrapped shavings, check the abrasive cloth or paper has no long ends that will be grabbed by the lathe.

A light touch is best for sanding, as pressure can cause friction-generated heat cracks in the workpiece. Spindlework in particular calls for gentle sanding, as the grain runs parallel to the lathe axis.

When hand sanding faceplate work, make sure you do it in 'safe' areas where the wood is rotating away from you, to avoid your sanding pad being flipped and your knuckles rapped.

These safe areas apply equally to ▶

power sanding operations, but the penalty for ignoring them is less severe than when doing it by hand.

Some turners swear by reverse sanding: reversing the rotation of the lathe so that wood fibres are not all lying in the same direction. 1f you use this option, make sure you don't unscrew your chuck from the lathe with work attached, as some hapless turners have.

Power sanding

When using power, sanding discs are supported on a soft pad, usually of composite rubber. Several systems are available, some with adhesive discs, some use Velcro, others use a twist-lock attachment. They can be used with either drills, grinders or air sanders.

We currently use the 'roloc' system, available from 3M stockists worldwide, for both the ease of interchanging different grit discs and for the longevity of the cloth-backed discs, which can be cleaned with crepe rubber sticks. Power-Lock and Quick-Lock are similar clip-on abrasive disc systems.

Pads come in different diameters, and we routinely use 50mm, 2" and 75mm, 3" in our work. A larger 150mm 6" pad we make up ourselves very cheaply, and it is excellent for large flat areas such as big platters.

There are also specialist finishing products such as the 'flapper' type also known as 'star wheels' which are useful for sanding hollow forms or uneven surfaced work.

Power sanding has had a mixed reception. When the early kits came out there was a lack of fine grits available, so we (and other woodworkers using this form of sanding) got into the habit of completing it by hand.

The reasons for continuing this practice no longer exist, as all grits are now freely available. Not only is there a huge range of conventional abrasive papers to choose from, but manufacturers have come up with extras such as non-woven nylon pads and buffing discs for fine polishing.

Most sanding is done with the work rotating on the lathe, but the piece can be stationary or even removed from the lathe altogether.

Removing all traces of a base for exhibition work is one occasion when you might do this, another is when you are making running repairs to a damaged 'masterpiece'.

A good tip here is to make a soft, yet firm, support for the workpiece by filling a plastic bag with shavings. This moulds to the piece, so it can be sanded without slipping.

Power sanding is, within reason, a boon, but used to excess it can blur the crisp edges of a piece and detract from a clear cut design.

High speed sanding

Contrary to much sanding lore, we have had consistently good results sanding at very high speeds (over 1200 RPM) with the lathe running at 1000 RPM, or faster.

This has become our chosen method, as it leaves a scratch-free finish on even the most recalcitrant 'picky' surface, including resin pock-

A 'flapper' or 'star' wheel of multilayered abrasive.

Cleaning a sanding disc with a crepe rubber stick.

ets and troublesome endgrain. Sanding is completed in a couple of passes over the work and no heat checks occur.

The pads used for high speed sanding are thinner than those for power sanding at lower speeds.

The downside is the cloud of fine dust you get. So, excellent as we find this method, it needs a workshop with an effective dust extractor. If you have one, do try it, as it works extremely well.

Hand v power

Though we are well aware that in many quarters hand sanding is felt to be more worthy than power, it's a preference hard to substantiate on results.

In blind trials, we've carried out sanding in three ways: by hand, power, and power followed by hand. Our 'panel' were unable to tell between the pieces finished by the different methods.

This suggests that if you want to save time and energy by using power-assisted sanding, you CAN achieve results equal to those you achieve by hand. ∎

Check your speed rating

Lathe speed 300 - 3,000 RPM	
Method of sanding	Typical RPM
Hand held	Reliant on lathe speed
Electric or air drill	Average RPM 2,000
Angle grinders	Average RPM 12,000
Air sanders	Average RPM 18,000

When using high speed sanding, check the sanding pad attachment is rated for the speed you want to use. The speed rating should be stamped on to the collar of the sanding pad.

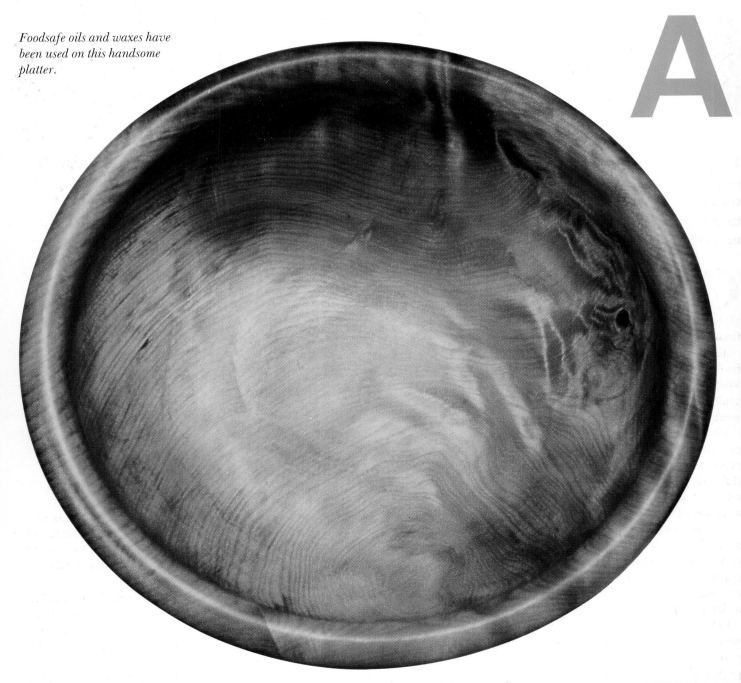

Foodsafe oils and waxes have been used on this handsome platter.

A

'Sadly, you can't slip on a quick coat of shellac and imagine you have a French polished piece of work'.

Turned domestic ware finished with foodsafe oils/waxes.

fine finish

In a follow-up article to their one on sanding, Bob and Ann Phillips turn to finishing, guiding woodturners through the bewildering array of products on offer.

Our sanding article on page 17 looks at how to prepare a smooth surface on your work. Here, we consider the options for the final finishing.

There's a bewildering array of finishing products to choose from. We'll review the main product groups available and briefly describe how they work and how to apply them.

First, let's look at oil and wax finishes. Although these are generally regarded as separate entities, the difference is only physical. A wax is just an oil which happens to be solid at room temperature.

We consider the two together to be suitable finishes for turned work coming into contact with food. A foam sponge can be used to apply the oil, or you might prefer a lint-free cloth or a clean paintbrush.

Oil/wax finish is very forgiving: if you find a minor imperfection on your work you can simply use abrasive paper to oil-sand the surface. Wipe the swarf away and then reapply your oil coating. Several coats should be buffed on, the more the merrier.

Soft wax can be applied in the same

Decorative burrs and delicate work lend themselves to penetrating-type finishes.

way, either separately or over an initial oil coating. If you use a hard block of wax to seal, apply oil first then hold the wax against the rotating work so it melts into the surface with the friction-generated heat.

There is a popular misconception that the harder the wax, the better and glossier the finish. In fact it's more a matter of relative molecular size, and appropriate soft waxes give a good finish and are much easier to apply.

For oil finishes, any food grade oil can be used, but select those which

don't readily oxidise (with accompanying rancid odours). The advertised 'healthy, polyunsaturated' types of salad or cooking oils such as safflower fit these criteria.

Walnut oil is particularly pleasant to use, if rather costly, while the common medicinal paraffin oil (also called mineral oil or liquid paraffin) is equally appropriate. True, it lacks the pleasant, nutty smell, but it's an effective, inexpensive option.

'Penetrating' oils

A popular example of the widely used penetrating oils and waxes are Danish oils. These are usually synthetic finishes, often containing chemicals to penetrate and combine with the wood in a process called polymerisation. They're applied in the same way as salad oils, with rag, sponge or brush.

The authors

Bob and Ann Phillips threw in good jobs nearly 10 years ago to become professional woodturners and have never looked back.
They supply shops and galleries throughout New Zealand and some of their pieces are in overseas collections. The couple have written a book on making money from woodturning, published by GMC Publications last year, and also wrote a three- part series for *Woodturning* on how to *Pump up the Profits*.

Applying a sealer to a vase. Note the mask to protect against spattering.

A good tip is to store the cloth or sponge applicator in a screwtop container. This avoids the risk of scratching your beautiful work with grit or wood chips held in dirty cloths.

The oil or resin soaks into the wood, hardening the surface fibres to create a tough and durable finish. This is useful for delicate work such as the decorative burr platters.

Sanding sealers

These are often used as a base for another finish, but can equally be a finishing coat in themselves. A simple method is to brush on the sealer with the lathe stopped.

Then, after a short interval to allow the sealer to dry, (this will vary with different sealers), re-start the lathe and sand or wire - wool the work.

Final coat

Finally, either re-apply a coat of the sealer or, if you prefer, use another product for the final coat. Sanding sealer can be used as a grain filler before applying a coat of oil or wax as described above.

Solid sticks are also available as grain filling agents in colours to match different woods. Most sealers are based on a cellulose lacquer mixed with stearate, so that when sanded between coats the abrasive will not clog up badly.

When sealer is applied to a vase, it is sanded after a brief drying period. Essentially, the sealer fills the pores in the wood, producing a smoother surface.

Varnishes

Modern varnishes are usually based on synthetics, including acrylics, alkyds and polyurethanes, which are by far the best known group. Boat building colleagues assure us that marine 'spa' varnishes still boast resin-oil mixes.

Whatever their composition, varnishes produce a hard surface which makes them an ideal finish for protecting decorated work. It's a tough coating that woodturners who make toys or games appreciate.

Although varnishes can be applied with brush or cloth, spraying is an easy and convenient application method for small items such as toys.

Spray cans

For small jobs, the proprietary spray cans are particularly convenient, but those planning a lot of spray finishes will probably gravitate towards a workshop spray system based on an air compressor, a subject in itself.

The solvents used in most varnishes usually take longer to evaporate than those used in lacquer and sealers. Fast drying varnishes have been developed though, and woodturners frustrated with long drying times can check out the market for these newer formulations.

Increasingly popular are catalytic sealer type finishes known variously as 'two pot lacquers', plastic coatings, or by a proprietary brand name.

The formulation comes in two seperate containers and the two parts are mixed together just before use. All have a limited shelf life when mixed, so have everything prepared before you start.

One part, usually called the hardener, is a chemical catalyst which, when added to the second part, speeds up the reaction between the two.

This reaction causes the mixture to rapidly 'cure' on the surface of the work to produce a very hard and usually glossy finish.

There are several mixtures, all with varying mixing proportions, so read the application instructions before use. After throughly mixing, these coatings are applied with a cloth and left for the manufacturers recommended period.

Disposable gloves should be worn to protect your hands. With the lathe re-started, the surface can be polished with a buffing pad or burnished with a handful of shavings.

If it seems too glossy, 'cut back' with a fine grade (000 or 0000) steel wool or other fine abrasive, to give a low lustre finish.

Many coatings can be applied with

Varnish produces a tough finish which can protect painted surfaces, as on decorated woodware.

other finishes. Soft wax, for example, could be used over a surface prepared in the way we've described.

A few may be incompatible, so check the product information on the container, preferably before purchase, but certainly before use.

Shellac finishes

Shellac is a traditional finish and reaches its height in a true French polish finish. Sadly, you can't slip on a quick coat of shellac and imagine you have a French polished piece of work. The 'real McCoy' is a tricky and time-consuming process.

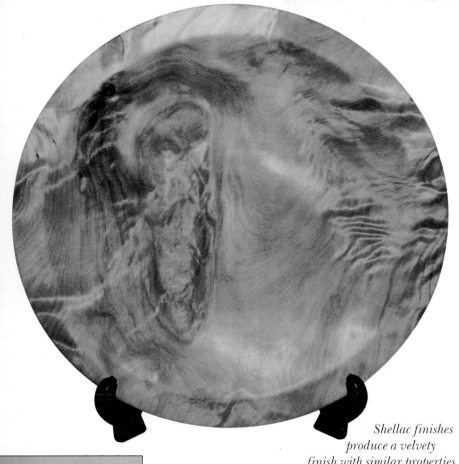

Shellac finishes produce a velvety finish with similar properties to the true French polish.

Two pot mixes of catalytic sealer produce a tough, impermeable surface which is very durable. If it seems too glossy, 'cut back' with a fine grade steel wool.

We haven't sufficient space here to discuss the relative merits of different grades of shellac, (which derives its name from the lac beetle), or of various 'cuts', rubbers, pumice and rottenstone combinations.

The shellac finish yields good, consistent results in a fraction of the time French polishing takes. If you want to learn the latter, it's a good starting point.

For a shellac finish it's worth spending time preparing the surface. You're not likely to be applying it to domestic ware, so work to the finer grits.

Applying the shellac mix is made easier if you use a weak dilution to start. We suggest 2:1 if using methylated spirits and shellac flakes, or a 20% distillation if using a proprietary solution.

To apply the shellac mix you can easily make a 'rubber' by wrapping cottonwool in a small lint-free cloth. Dab the applicator in your mix and, with the piece stationary on the lathe, lightly apply the shellac.

A light oil

Next, wipe over with a light oil. Mineral oil or walnut are the ones we prefer. It doesn't hurt to spin the work at this stage to ensure even coverage.

Finally, work over the piece with a fine wire wool (000 or 0000). You can repeat these basic steps to 'build up' a deeper finish.

The whole process takes minutes rather than the hours or more you will spend preparing the true French polished finish. This compromise gives a pleasing low-lus-

tre finish with similar properties.

We save the real thing for special pieces and always feel the effort to be justified by the incomparable velvety finish.

To conclude, the skill needed to apply a true French polish takes considerable effort to acquire, but is immensely satisfying and well worth doing.

Safety considerations

Whatever finish you choose, be well-informed. Read the product literature of any new finish you buy. Product names can be misleading and may give no clue to the additives, which may be incompatible with your intended use.

Keep in mind, that many products have been developed for uses other than turnery. Check the fine print on the glossy brochure (back page, miniscule type) and you'll find the disclaimers can be sweepingly thorough.

Thus, abrasion resistance, durability and ease of maintenance is fulsomely extolled but product suitability for food contact is left out. So don't assume, check up.

Turned work in domestic use is subjected to treatments that can disrupt the finish used. Will any 'nasties' leach out under acidic conditions created by some salad dressings? When the surface is scraped by salad servers and cutlery, are scrapings of the hard surface coating removed?

There's also your safety to consider. Solvent-soaked rags left on workshop benches have been the cause of several fires. If you're not in the habit of disposing of applicator cloths after use, keep them well sealed.

Store flammable finishes safely. Check your working area is well-ventilated and ensure you don't inhale any volatile solvents contained in your finishes.

The subject of finishes is an extensive one. Here we have given you an overall perspective, with some pointers to the pros and cons of the different ones available. ■

Turn a sculpture

Why not be a bit more imaginative and create a sculpture from your turnings, as Jonathan Merrett did for his garden.

Fence

First design idea.

The turned sculpture in place on my garden fence.

An 'architectural feature' was what we needed, the landscape gardener told us, when we had our garden redesigned. It would serve as a focal point. Visions of concrete gnomes and bird baths flashed before my eyes.

But then I began to wonder whether I might not be able to turn something interesting for that part of the garden.

I had the idea of having a sculpture 'grow', like a plant, out of the garden fence, to the side of our sitting area, and the design blossomed from there. I eventually settled on the shape of the hellebore plant and drew my first design.

I now knew the main part of the turning was going to be the creation of a number of bowl like shapes, of various sizes. I didn't want them to look too 'finished'.

I got the timber for my sculpture from the woodpile outside the back door. It was well-weathered, having lain there for two years. Most of it was oak, beech and ash.

I took logs with a diameter and length of between 100-150mm, 4-6" and split them down the middle. Holding them between centres I

A variety of shapes were turned.

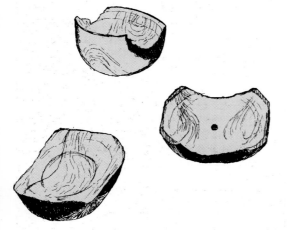

turned the outside of each shape, including a spigot for holding them in the Masterchuck when reversed.

Reversing each piece, I hollowed out the interior. The finished nature was determined by the wood. Some were left with a rim of bark, some were shallow, others deep. Some were square-edged, others round.

I didn't sand, but in some cases the tool finishing was smooth, while in others I left ridges. Every shape is different and hopefully this reflects the variety and randomness of nature.

Each piece was again reversed and held against a wooden faceplate by the revolving centre. The spigot was removed with a skew

▶

'Every shape is different and hopefully this reflects the variety and randomness of nature'.

chisel as the tailstock was gradually wound in, maintaining pressure on the workpiece.

Having turned the shapes, the creation of the sculpture itself was a matter of trial and error. I half cut out a 'stalk' shape with the bandsaw and turned a spigot on the end while it could still be held in the lathe.

I completed the bandsawing and spoke-shaved the stalk into a tapering, round shape. The largest shape was attached to this by a hole drilled into the base and secured with waterproof glue.

The connecting stalks were turned out of scrap softwood. Their length was determined by holding up the shape against the sculpture and trying out a variety of combinations and positions.

All the stalks were left with a spigot on both ends. I used a hand held electric drill to drill the holes in the shapes, so their angles could be varied and correspond to the positions decided upon by the above process.

Two main stalks

As the sculpture grew, I decided to have two main stalks protruding from the fence. I also put in short stalks with no shape on the end and placed a bud at the base of the sculpture.

The finished piece was quite different to my original drawing (as you can see), but that was part of the fun of making it. It ended up 760mm, 30" high and stands out from the fence by about 380mm, 15".

While still in the workshop, I turned the sculpture upside down in the vice so the underside could be varnished. When dry, I fastened the sculpture to the fence and painted it with yacht varnish.

The varnish was laid on heavily and allowed to 'puddle' in the hollows. This adds extra texture and interest to the shapes.

Water, too, collects in the hollows and overflows from shape to shape, falling attractively in steps to the ground. I tested it with the hosepipe, so I know it works.

Of course, to appreciate this best would mean standing out in the rain. So I'm happy to remember how it was with the hose. ■

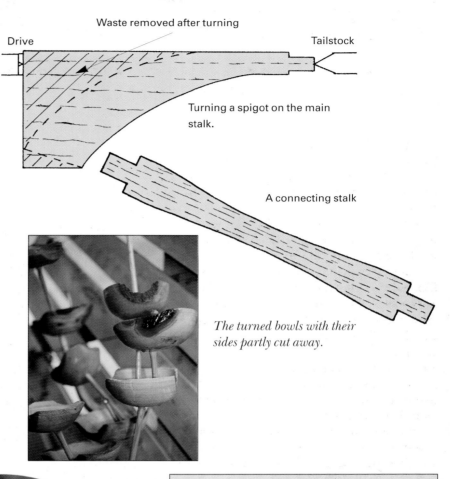

Waste removed after turning

Drive

Tailstock

Turning a spigot on the main stalk.

A connecting stalk

The turned bowls with their sides partly cut away.

The side positioning of this piece allows rain water to overflow from bowl to bowl.

The author

Jonathan Merrett is a musician by training and a teacher by profession, currently working at a middle school in Warwickshire. He learnt to turn by reading books, seeing demonstrations at shows and through hard experience.

Jonathan sees woodturning as a rewarding and relaxing recreation. Being interested in painting and sketching, he welcomes the opportunity that turning provides to be creative three dimensionally. He enjoys sharing his interests with anyone who will listen and with the children he teaches – who have to listen! Jonathan hopes his young son will follow in his steps and be practically creative.

Mike Pearn describes a system he developed to overcome the health hazard of fine wood dust in the workshop

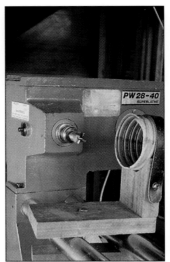

DUST BUSTER

The air-intake hose attached to the helmet of the face visor.

Having listened to a talk on the health hazards of inhaling fine wood dust, I decided to protect myself. At first I used a simple dust mask, but this gave little protection, impaired breathing and misted my spectacles.

Switching to the cartridge filter type of mask was an improvement, but it too was uncomfortable. So I tried out several respirator helmets.

These gave a flow of apparently clean air between my face and the visor, making breathing more comfortable and overcoming misting, but they were expensive – not only to buy, but also to run, as they needed replacement filters. And battery charging was irksome.

I concluded that the products available tried to contain the dust problem rather than curing it at source. A radical rethink was required.

I installed a dust extractor system – a 100mm, 4in intake tube mounted on a simple 'banjo' arrangement, which allowed me to move it along the bed bars behind the work.

This was a huge improvement, drastically cutting the cloud of dust I normally stood in. But two problems remained.

Danger

One was that well known by users of bag-filter dust extractors, where fine dust – the dangerous particles – escape back into the atmosphere through the sides of the cloth bag.

The same problem occurs with filters in helmet respirators. If air gets through the filter, so do some fine dust particles.

The second problem was that sucking dust is not as efficient as blowing it away. Test it for yourself with a straw and a table-tennis ball. A strong puff through the

▶

straw will blow the ball away even when it is some distance from it, but you will have to suck hard to move the ball towards the straw.

The obvious answer to the first of these problems was to move the extractor outside the workshop, taking the 100mm, 4in hose through the wall. I kept the total length of hose as short as possible to avoid reducing the extractor's efficiency.

Moving the extractor outside solved the problem of fine dust escaping from the bag-filter into the work

The air-intake hose is suspended from the workshop ceiling.

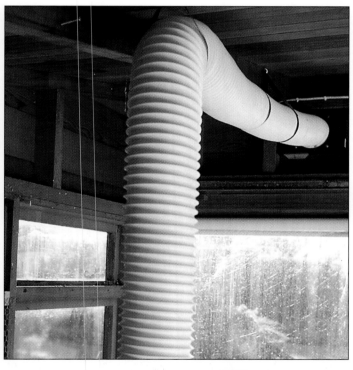

The complete system, showing the visor with air-intake hose attached, hanging on a handy hook, ready for use. Note the extractor hose has been taken through the workshop wall.

area, but I was left with the problem that sucking dust away is not very efficient.

However, while moving the extractor, I noticed draughts were entering the workshop from gaps around doors and windows and realised that, if I was not to create a vacuum in the workshop, the air sucked out had to be replaced. Hence the draughts.

All I needed to do was to control the inflow and use it to blow dust from the workplace towards the extractor intake hose.

After placing a draught excluder strip around windows and doors, I fitted an inlet grill at the top of a wall away from the external extractor.

From the grill, I suspended a 100mm, 4in hose over the workpiece and directed a curtain of air over the work towards the extractor intake hose. This greatly improved dust collection.

The main drawback of the system was that windows and doors had to be properly sealed in order to have a good airflow over the workpiece. If a door or window was left open the flow was cut significantly or stopped altogether.

So help with the airflow was needed. The solution was to install a fan at the intake grill. I found a shower cubicle fan to be ideal, being designed to fit in a 100mm, 4in duct.

With this installed I could use my dust removal system with windows and doors open – a must during hot weather.

One hot day, I realised that the airflow over the workpiece was a cool breeze of *fresh air* from outside the workshop, *free from wood dust.*

Final change

So the final modification to my system was to attach a connector to the helmet part of my flip-up face visor. This allowed the end of the hose from the fan unit to be fitted to the top of the helmet.

A small deflector was devised to direct a steam of clean fresh down the inside of the visor. The result – no misting-up of spectacles and dust-free air to breathe.

For mobility and comfort inside the visor helmet, I used lightweight, plastic, flexible hose (of the kind used to ventilate shower cubicles) from the top of the fan unit to the top of the helmet.

You get this hose, and the connector for attaching it to the helmet, from large DIY stores. The lightweight hose is suspended from the workshop ceiling.

Although my system may make you look like an astronaut on a spacewalk, this is a small price to pay for breathing clean, fresh air and drastically cutting the health risk from inhaling fine wood dust. ■

In Part One of this two-part article, Geoff Heath describes how he put his woodturning techniques to good effect by making display stands for buttonhooks.

Since few people under the age of 40 seem to know what a button-hook is, let me begin this article on how to make a buttonhook display stand, with a word of explanation.

In the days before the zip-fasteners, ladies wore gloves, boots and dresses with long rows of buttons. To help them pass these awkward little things through their corresponding buttonholes, the buttonhook was invented.

This consisted of a tapered steel shank with a hook at the slender end and a handle at the other. Today, they're looked upon as collectable antiques.

A friend of mine asked me to make a display stand for her buttonhook collection. She sketched out what she had in mind and even lent me a few precious hooks so I could decide the stand's dimensions.

Button - shaped feet

The finished job consisted of two circular discs separated by a short central pillar and topped by a finial. The lower disc stood on three button-shaped feet, so that any warping of the disc would not affect the stand's stability.

The upper disc was drilled with 12 holes for the shanks, and the lower one had shallow depressions (ie partly drilled holes) in which the hooks rested. The whole assembly was glued together.

My friend liked the stand and asked if I could make it as a 'flat pack', so other members of the Buttonhook Society (which I'd never heard of) could order them.

And order them they did, after a mention in the society's newsletter. I offered

The dummy faceplates. The cork face is screwed to the blank, and the metal faceplate is then screwed into the hollowed side. The pegs ensure concentricity.

The two sizes of button hook stands and one set of component parts.

GETTING H

the stand in either 'light' or 'dark' woods and had modified them. The central pillar was now hollow, with a 'spine' which had a threaded end, making it easy to assemble the parts.

The upper and lower discs were made from blanks about 50mm, 2" thick, which I found was enough for three discs. After cutting each one slightly oversize on the bandsaw, I mounted it with double-sided adhesive tape to the faceplate and cleaned up the exposed face, ensuring it was perfectly flat.

I drilled a 12mm, ½" DIA hole ½" deep into the blank, using the tailstock to hold the drill chuck. The face was then sanded and finished with melamine polish and steel wool.

The perimeter was left 'as sawn', experience having taught that the sticky tape

Tapping the hole in a lower disc. The work is locked in position while the tap and tailstock are advanced by hand.

A disc being sawn from the blank which is still on the faceplate. A cradle stops the work rolling during the cut.

was not always strong enough to cope with gouge-work on the rim of the disc.

So, for subsequent operations, I used screws for safe attachment. The problem was how to disguise the holes by which the upper and lower discs were screwed to the faceplate.

Those who recall my 'Widgets and Wheezes' article (*Woodturning*, Issues 10 and 11, now reprinted in *Woodturning Techniques*) will not be surprised to learn that I made several tools and jigs to simplify production.

Four dummy faceplates, each consisting of a wooden disc placed between the faceplate and the workpiece, were the first of these tools.

To ensure repeated concentricity, each dummy was recessed to fit snugly over the faceplate proper, and held in place by screws.

I placed three countersunk holes in the dummy at equal intervals around a pitch surface of the same diameter as that for the holes which would later be drilled to take the buttonhooks.

Small diameter screws held the 'clean' side of the blank against the dummy, which had a cork facing. While the pilot holes for these were being drilled, I centred the dummy on the blank with a removeable 12mm, ½" DIA peg.

The assembly was then mounted on the lathe. In the finished stands the holes for the buttonhooks removed any trace

of the holes for the retaining screws.

Now the rough exposed face was cleaned up and the blank turned to the required diameter, care being taken to produce a true cylinder. My blank was going to produce either one upper disc and two lower, or two upper and one lower.

Thus, two blanks would give me enough discs for three stands. The disc now against the dummy was always an upper one. The outermost one could be either an upper or a lower. The one sandwiched between them was always a lower.

My next job was to drill a hole part way through the centre of the blank. If the disc was to be an upper one, the hole would be 12mm, ½" DIA and ½" deep. If a lower disc, it would be 10mm, ⅜" DIA and 25mm, 1" deep, and would then be threaded, using a 12mm, ½" tap.

For this operation I locked the lathe spindle, and the tap was supported at its free end by the revolving centre, so keeping it in line with the pilot hole.

By advancing the tailstock with one

'My friend liked the stand and asked if I could make it as a "flat-pack", so other members of the Buttonhook Society could order them'.

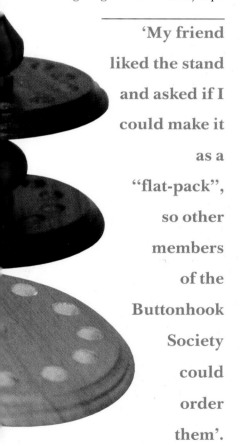

OOKED

The bandsawing cradle (left) and push stick have sandpaper gripping patches.

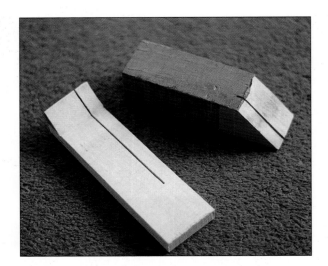

Below: The drilling jig in operation. The peg is placed in the first hole drilled to stop the jig rotating.

Bottom: A 'gang' of three feet turned together

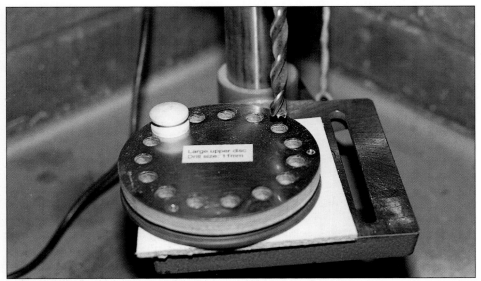

exposed face had to be cleaned up to leave a disc of the right thickness (10mm, ⅜") before the edge was turned to a classical pattern.

After sanding and polishing, this disc was removed from the dummy faceplate and set aside. If there was a second upper disc in this batch of three, it was mounted on the dummy and finished in the same way.

The lower discs had a slightly different dummy faceplate, as the central hole was tapped, needing a threaded peg to centre the blank on the dummy, which had a corresponding tapped hole. Otherwise, the procedure was exactly the same as for the upper discs.

Now it was time to drill the circle of holes in the discs. I made two drill jigs for each size of stand: one for the upper and one for the lower disc.

The jigs were plywood circles, faced with sheet brass to reduce wear in the holes, and drilled with a ring of holes at the right pitch diameter. The large jigs had 15 holes and the smaller, 12.

Central spigot

I located the jigs on the discs with a central spigot. For the upper disc this was a 12mm, ½" DIA peg, and the disc was rotated on the jig until the three small screw holes lined up with three holes in the jig.

The holes were bench-drilled using a lip-and-spur bit to ensure a clean hole. Once the spur had gone through the disc, I stopped drilling, so preventing jagged 'break-out' had the hole been completed in one go.

The first hole drilled in each disc was pegged to the drilling jig to prevent any relative rotation. When all the holes had been drilled part-way through, the disc was removed from the jig, turned over and back-drilled to give a crisp edge to both sides of the holes.

The jig for the lower discs had a central spigot consisting of a short length of threaded dowel, on to which the disc was screwed. I drilled shallow holes, using a normal twist drill, so producing conical recesses.

The three screw holes from the faceplate mounting were, of course, on the

hand while turning the tap with the other, I achieved successful tapping every time. Removing the faceplate assembly from the lathe, I sliced off the first disc on the bandsaw.

This may sound a tricky operation, but it was safe, because I pressed the face of the blank against the fence and used a special cradle with a sandpaper-covered

wedge to prevent the blank rotating.

The push stick was another sandpaper-covered wedge. The separated disc was set aside and the faceplate assembly returned to the lathe.

I repeated this operation to produce a second half-finished disc and was left with enough material for a third. The central hole was already drilled, but the

The drive spigot fitted into the hole drilled through the central column.

A central column mounted between the drive spigot and a live centre in the tailstock.

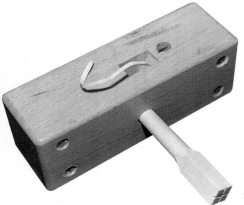

Threading the spine. The square end which provides grip for this operation was later turned to fit into the finial.

underside of the disc. The three feet were turned from one piece of wood, being separated after removal from the lathe, and finished by hand.

They were mushroom-shaped and their shanks were glued into 10mm, ⅜" DIA holes drilled in the underside of the lower discs, using the dummy faceplate screw holes as centres.

The stand's central column was a simple piece of spindle turning, a 12mm, ½" DIA hole being drilled the length of the work as the first operation on the lathe.

The workpiece was subsequently driven by means of a tapered spigot mounted in a chuck, the spigot being jammed into the central hole.

The finial was a similar piece of spindle turning, but with a 12mm, ½" DIA hole drilled only part-way down the centre. The threaded 'spine' which held the stand together, fitted into this hole.

The spine was a piece of hardwood (beech and holly proved excellent for this) turned down to 12mm, ½" DIA, leaving one end square.

Using this square end as a grip, I threaded the other end in a Sarjent's box.

After making sure the thread ran smoothly into the lower disc, I turned the square end down and glued-in the finial. The stand was now complete.

The secretary of the Buttonhook Society sent me parcels of ready-addressed Jiffy bags and I posted the 'flat packs' off to their new owners. I was amazed at the destinations: New York, South Africa, Holland. Altogether, I made 57 stands.

Eventually the orders petered out, but the Buttonhook Society hasn't finished with me yet, as you'll discover in Part Two of this article (on page 37). ∎

A complete 'flat pack' button hook stand ready for postal delivery.

The author

Geoff Heath is an amateur turner and a founder member of the High Peak Woodturners, now part of the Northern Federation of Woodturning Groups.
He edits *The Circular,* the High Peak newsletter. Now retired from the aircraft industry where he spent 44 years of his working life, he divides his spare time between his lathe and his computer, which he has programmed to draw crossword grids – skew symmetric ones of course!
Two of Geoff's previous articles for *Woodturning* (Widgets and Wheezes and Inside Out) describe various techniques he adopted to overcome specific problems or to produce special effects. He describes here how he put these techniques to use to make display stands for buttonhooks.

To the point

The round point tool, now being manufactured by Crown Tools of Sheffield as the Three Point Tool, is a beginners' dream, as **Ron Fernie** reports

Cutting a groove with the Three Point Tool, the point is pushed in to the wood with one facet upwards.

Rolling the right side of a bead. Two grooves have been cut and the tool is rolled and sweeps from the right-hand groove to the crest of the bead.

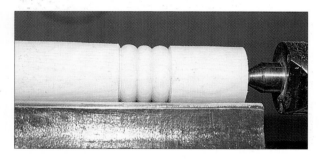

Three beads from the Three Point Tool in Spanish chestnut *(Aesculus hippocastanum)*.

Facing off the endgrain. The upper bevel is near level and tilted a little to the left.

The round point tool which Bill Jones wrote about in Issue 4 of Woodturning, is now being made by Crown Tools, of Sheffield. It's called the Three Point Tool, but many people don't seem to know what it's for or how to use it.

Yet it is a user-friendly tool that can enable even beginners to form beads on spindle and faceplate work (and to dress end grain) with less than 10 minutes practice.

Freedom

This tool will free many from the sometimes long, frustrating and (at times) heart-stopping process of getting to grips with the skew chisel.

To start, they may think it was simply beginners' luck when they finish forming their first perfect bead. For those who have experienced the 'bite' of a skew will find it hard to accept how docile the Three Point Tool is, with no dig-ins.

When forming beads in face-plate work, the tool will not dig or skate, while allowing perfect control. There is nothing more frustrating than, when nearing completion of a nice piece of work, you have the top ripped off a bead by a bead-forming tool.

I'll start to describe how to use the tool on a bead, a common fly in the ointment.

Start with a 50mm, 2in diameter cylinder of wood between centres. Set the tool-rest as for normal spindle turning, so that the tool operates just above centre height.

With one flat bevel uppermost and parallel to the bed bars, and the tool at 90° to the lathe axis, line the handle up on your shirt buttons. If you have no shirt buttons, just stand so that it is right below your nose, not to one side of the tool, as for other tools.

Push the tool forward to make a V-cut with the point. Move it 10mm, ⅜in to the right and repeat, then twist the handle to the left while slowly lowering it and swinging it across your stomach to the left. Don't drag the edge over the wood. Try to leave the point behind and for bigger beads change the pivot point on the rest and repeat passes as required.

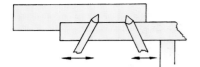

Planing cut.

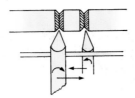

Bead forming, seen from above.

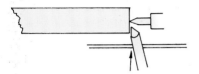

Endgrain planing.

Three Point Tool manipulation

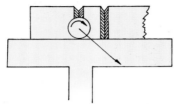

Bead forming seen from
end of handle.

Endgrain after the facing cut from the Three Point Tool.

Planing with the Three Point Tool. The point is clear of the wood and cutting starts at the middle of the edge.

Rolling a bead on face work is similar to the spindle beads, here a rolling sweep to the right.

Beads shaped, the finish is from the tool.

After the right-hand side of the bead has been formed, move the tool to the left-hand V-cut, twisting, lowering and swinging the tool to the right to form a perfect bead. If not, a little more practice will soon put it right.

Facing endgrain

That done, make sure your toolrest is positioned so you can safely work on the end grain at the tailstock end of the cylinder.

With one facet, flat bevel uppermost and slightly tilted to the left, and the left-hand edge at 90° to the lathe axis, push the tool towards the centre while slowly lifting the handle.

The whole of the edge will be in contact. It will be docile and won't dig in – ideal for cutting shoulders or dressing the flat tops and bottoms of boxes.

There you have it! The only thing I forgot to mention is that you may find the tool chattering through lack of familiarity when you are forming a bead.

This is easily corrected by placing your index finger under the toolrest and clamping the tool to the rest with the ball of your thumb to form a fixed pivot point.

Start a planing cut with the handle well down and to the right (if you are right-handed). At the same time, have an edge tilted to the right, so that it's mid-point is in contact with the work.

Try this with the lathe stopped and draw the tool along the rest to the right, producing a fine shaving. Fire up the lathe, and away you go.

First, move the tool to the left from the tailstock end, then (without changing angles) draw it back to the right. You will find the tool works well in both directions.

Race along

At first, you may find the tool wants to race along the rest, but change the angle of attack and you will soon have it under control. Dressing fillets I'll leave to you, and your ingenuity to find other uses for the tool.

If all this is still not clear, you can call me Monday-Friday (before 5pm) on 01828 686106. Or, if you are passing the Scottish Antique & Arts Centre in Abernyte, Perthshire, you can always pop in and see me. As Bob Hoskins says, "It's good to talk". ■

New forms for old

'Just as a Picasso, Kandinsky or Mondriaan analyses shape or form, why shouldn't a woodturner use his imagination to create something other than salad bowls..'

*Oak sculptural form, 220mm 8 ¾"
DIA x 260mm
10 ¼" H.*

Embellishments are all very well, but why not free the imagination completely and create new, sculptural forms, from traditional shapes, argues distinguished Belgian turner Professor Daniel Ellegiers.

Many woodturners seem to find it hard to escape from the traditional basic shapes of bowls, platters, goblets and boxes. You only have to visit exhibitions around the world or read woodturning magazines and books to see the truth of this.

As most of these basic shapes go back to Roman pottery and beyond, and few, if any, new ones can be found, creative woodturners try to disguise them by adding frills.

Art Deco

These may be pleasantly reminiscent of Art Deco frivolities. But instead of hiding or negating basic shapes, as

▶

Traditional shapes built up into something unusual, 220mm 8 ¾" DIA x 150mm 6" H.

A piece shaped like a platter, but with a difference, 220mm 8 ¾" DIA x 240mm 9 ½" H.

This bowl was split at the sides and would normally have been thrown away. I filled the splits with putty and glued then painted a piece over the rim to hide its irregular oval shape. It measures 310mm 12 ¼" DIA x 120mm 4 ¾" H.

The author

Prof Dr Daniel Ellegiers, 74, was born in Westrozebeke, Belgium, and is a man of wide education and experience. His studies have included humanities, history of art, archeology, Chinese and Japanese language and literature – and furniture making. He is a Doctor of Philosophy and Literature.

He received several bursaries for scientific research during his early career, and was a lecturer at the University of Osaka, Japan, in the early 1950s before returning to take professorships at universities in Belgium.

He was Deputy Commissioner-General of the Belgian Government from 1969-71, lecturer at the NATO College in Rome in the early 1970s, and Professor at the War College, Brussels from 1975-89.

In retirement Prof Ellegiers enjoys teaching and demonstrating woodturning, as well as producing his own work at his home in Gavere-Vurste, Belgium.

Sectionalising a piece can turn it into something completely different, 220mm 8 ¾" DIA x 260mm 10 ⅜" H.

dominant traditional forms and from the limitations of the lathe, which always turns in the round.

Questions

Before starting work on a piece, ask yourself questions like these: What can I do with the shape of a bowl, platter, cylinder or cone? Why don't I cut up a platter and glue the pieces together again in such a way that a new shape is created? Must I stick to a bowl or platter which is functional?

Just as a Picasso, Kandinsky or Mondriaan analyses shape or form, why shouldn't a woodturner use his imagination to create something other than salad bowls etc? After all, woodturning is about creating forms, discovering, and inventing.

Sculptural turning, or formwriting as it's also called, is a move towards geometric shapes and abstraction, changing old forms into new.

It challenges normal perceptions, inviting viewers to share in the creative experience of the turner by considering such things as the shifting of light on a piece, the interaction of colour and texture and the effect of shadows.

It's theoretical, aesthetic, intellectual – and fun. ∎

Geometric form, 160mm 6 ¼" DIA x 160mm 6 ¼" H

though you're ashamed of their simplicity (or of not being able to find new ones), why not try to use these age old forms in a new, sculptural way?

Doing this offers an escape from

'To prevent unscrupulous collectors passing off these buttonhooks as "antiques", I would need to make them distinctive, but clearly not Victorian'.

HOOKED ON HANDLES

In Part Two of his article on buttonhooks, Geoff Heath tells how he made more than 100 unique handles for these implements to mark the 15th birthday of the Buttonhooks Society.

In Part One, on page 28, I told you how I became involved with the Buttonhook Society through my buttonhook display stand. Now I'm going to tell you how I came to make a batch of special buttonhook handles for the society.

The story starts about two years ago, when the society bought up the entire stock of buttonhook shanks from the Sheffield firm which had made them for 60 years or so.

The society's 15th anniversary was coming up, and sales secretary Sue Brandon asked me if I would make souvenir handles for these shanks. I readily agreed.

Then she explained that to prevent unscrupulous collectors passing off these buttonhooks as 'antiques,' I would need to make them distinctive, but clearly not Victorian.

Faced with this problem, I made three trial handles. One was a straight-forward piece of spindle turning. The second an example of 'two-centre' turning, the free end being oval in section while the shank end was circular.

My third handle was the society's favourite. This was an 'inside-out' handle with a captive spindle visible inside the 'windows', much on the lines of the 'mother and baby' lace bobbins described by John Fisher in Woodturning, Issue 30.

My own article on 'inside-out' turning in Issue 28 described the basic technique I adopted, but I made a few modifications for simplicity's sake.

I made a display board for the Buttonhook Society's annual meeting, as many members wanted to know how the spindle got inside the handle.

The captive spindle was free to rotate, and round it was wrapped an 'able-label', bearing a message about the society's anniversary.

This label was the key to the age of the buttonhook, and I had to be sure the windows were big enough for it to be read easily, but small enough not to be removed without destroying the handle.

▶

Top: Display board, showing the stages in making the buttonhook handles.
Above: A pair of finished spindles, together with the 'go/no go' gauge.

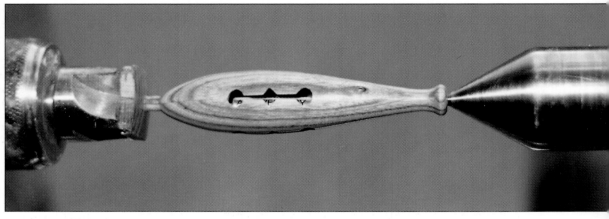

I made the spindle in pairs from 8mm, 5⁄16" square stock, using a bobbin drive. Each 'able-label' was 19mm, 3⁄4" wide, which meant the spindle had to be of about 6mm, 1⁄4" DIA.

Anything less than this resulted in an overlap of the label's edges, which could have led to it peeling back, while much more than 6mm left an unsightly gap.

I therefore made a 'go/no go' gauge (a piece of sheet brass with 6.5¼" and 6mm 15⁄64", holes drilled through it). A spindle had to pass easily through the larger hole, but not enter the smaller.

Having passed the sizing test, the spindle pairs were separated and posted in batches to the society's secretary, who fitted the labels. While waiting for the spindles' return, I got on with the inside work.

Contrary to my earlier thoughts, I found there was no need to 'true-up' the faces of the blank. For jobs of this size (22mm, 7⁄8" square x 90mm, 3 ½" long) the 'as sawn' surfaces were quite adequate.

I sawed the block into four smaller squares, and these were rotated 'corners-to-centre before being glued together into a new blank. Using Hot Stuff gap-filling superglue, I produced sound joints every time, very quickly.

Before sawing the blocks into quarters, it was essential to label one end, eg ABCD. Otherwise, once the four pieces had been cut, there was no way of telling how they should be re-arranged, except for the grain pattern.

If my arithmetic is correct, there are more than 98,000 ways of re-assembling the four bits.

At this stage the reconstituted blank had its outer surfaces smoothed by holding it against a belt sander. I checked to ensure the final shape was a perfectly square block.

Just above the belt I fixed a wooden fence, against which one surface could be pressed while I sanded the adjacent one, so giving me a right angle between 'face' and 'edge'.

Diagonal saw cuts across each end of

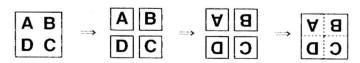

Labelling, sawing, rotating and re-assembling the components of a handle blank.

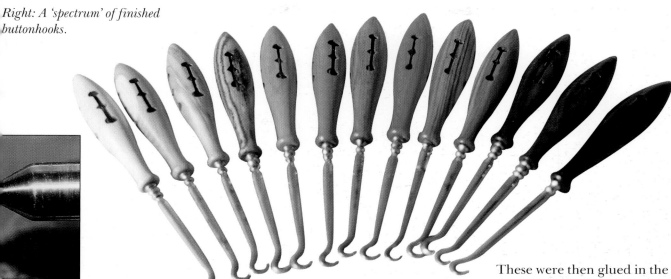

Right: A 'spectrum' of finished buttonhooks.

Below: A batch of blanks.

the blank located the centres. It didn't matter if the glue-lines didn't quite intersect at these centres. What DID matter was that the saw cuts passed through the corners of the blank and would meet at the centre when the four parts were re-assembled for the second turning.

At one end of the blank I drilled a small hole to take the point of the four-pronged driving centre, which then fitted snugly into the saw cuts with no tendency to split the joints.

At the other end, where at one time I would have used a ring centre, I found a revolving centre worked perfectly well.

A simple pattern was turned in the middle of the blank. Rather than think up a new pattern every time, I devised a standard one for all handles.

After finishing and polishing this area, I sawed the blank along the glue lines into the four constituent squares.

These were then glued in the original configuration, taking care to line up the ends of the windows.

At each end of the blank the intersection of the diagonal saw cuts automatically coincided with the intersection of the glue lines, though the blank's outer surfaces were likely to have some 'small steps' along the lengthwise glue lines. These steps were, of course, removed during final turning.

I inserted the spindle in the handle during this final gluing stage, making sure no glue got on the spindle. Before the final turning started, I drilled the blank at the driving end as before and drilled a stepped hole on the lathe from the tailstock end to take the tapered tang of the shank.

The spindles rattled about inside the handles while the outside was being turned, but they never came to any harm.

I had a free hand in the choice of the wood and used a wide range of exotic timbers, always ensuring that those in each batch of 12 were of different colours. I must confess that, although I started each batch with a dozen blanks, I was lucky if more than 10 survived the full cycle of operations.

I made over 100 handles and fixed them to the shanks with Hot Stuff. Each buttonhook in my 'spectrum' was supplied with a certificate of authenticity. I'm the proud owner of Certificate No 001, being allowed by the society to keep one as a souvenir. ■

Kai Kothe, of Kelkheim, Germany, teaches electrical engineering and English in vocational training. His interests in technology and English took him, in 1980, to the Centre for Alternative Technology, in Machynlleth, Powys, Wales, where he has since returned several times as a volunteer worker. The centre had a small woodturning lathe on which Kai 'played around' after work, during his first visit. He soon became hooked on woodturning.

Back in Germany, he bought a lightweight second-hand lathe which handled turning between centres quite well.

The availability of green wood after severe storms led to him experimenting with this kind of turning, and to his converting a heavier metal-turning lathe for turning wood.

Kai enjoys woodworking and woodturning as a spare-time activity which, thanks to magazines like *Woodturning* and many English books on the subject, also allows him to brush up his English.

He is 33 years old and is married with a young son.

KAI KOTHE

Here's how to make a complete set of accessories for your scroll chuck.

Photo 1 A small bowl is held in the adjustable chuck for finishing the base.

Customise

Normally, there are no problems with balanced and centred bowls, but any uneven mass distribution can cause heavy vibrations. Therefore it helps to have a heavy lathe which can be operated at low speeds until you are sure higher speeds won't cause trouble.

Construction

Fixing the four 15mm ⅝" plywood segments to the wood jaw plates and drilling the holes for the rubber stops requires precision engineering in wood.

I used an ordinary hand-held electric drill mounted in an inexpensive drill stand for drilling the holes, but spent a lot of time marking their exact positions.

Most makers and distributors of scroll chucks (like the Nova, Craft Supplies' new multi-grip 2000, the Vantage, Robot Premier, Multistar, Masterchuck, and Axminster chucks) offer additional wood jaw plates or cole jaws for them.

Here are some ideas on how to build custom-made cole jaws using wood jaw plates and how to make accessories for these and ready-made cole jaws.

The basic chuck

Photo 1 shows a small bowl held in the chuck for finishing the base. This kind of chuck can be adjusted easily to hold different sizes of bowls by moving the rubber stops into the appropriate position.

The scroll mechanism allows a very firm grip on the bowl when the chuck is tightened. The maximum bowl diameter that can be mounted – in my case 400mm 15 ¾" – is determined by the construction of the lathe and the recommendations of the chuck manufacturer.

Fixing the wood jaw plates

First you round the four-square plywood segments on the bandsaw and then fix them to the wood jaw plates. When the chuck is fully closed the plates should touch each other, but there should be a little gap of 1 or 2mm between the wooden segments.

This gap is needed because it's difficult to position the wood jaw plates exactly into the corners of the wooden segments. Put several layers of sticky tape around the corners of these segments and align the surface of the tape with the wood jaw plates to determine the gap.

I marked the position of the screws by using a pointed wood-drill bit of the same diameter as the holes in the wood

'It helps to have a heavy lathe which can be operated at low speeds until you are sure higher speeds won't cause trouble.'

jaw plates. If you use wood-screws to fix the wood jaw plates, pre-drill the screwholes.

Because most woodscrews are tapered and only the thicker part of the screw will grip in the pre-drilled holes, I used screws too long for the job and ground the protruding end away. Only remove one screw at a time for shortening.

Trimming

When you put the four segments into your scroll chuck, you might find it isn't possible to close the chuck completely because the wooden segments touch each other before the wood jaw plates touch.

This can be overcome by enlarging the gap between the

or scrollsaw cut (Photo 2).

Photos 2 and 3 were taken at a later stage, when the holes had already been drilled. Cut carefully, without removing the wood jaw plates.

Maximum safe jaw travel

Before you start the layout of the holes for the rubber stops you have to find out the maximum safe travel of your jaws. Open the chuck until jaw No 4 can be taken out. Now watch the scroll and tighten the chuck again.

Let the end of the scroll travel through the visible opening and turn the key a little further for added safety. Now you can measure the maximum safe

distance between the wood jaw plates.

If you saw a piece of wood to this width you can always check this distance later on.

Distance of rubber stops

Close the chuck completely and mount it on the lathe to true the rim. Measure the overall diameter in the closed and open position of the chuck and divide the difference between the two measurements by two.

The result tells you how to space the centres of the holes for the rubber stops. If it is possible to position them about 2mm closer to each other without weakening the segments

too much, you should do so.

This overlap makes the later use of the chuck more convenient. If you can't space the holes as described, you can drill the holes further apart and use stops of different sizes.

Position of holes

Close the chuck completely, put it on the lathe and fix a piece of cardboard with double-sided tape to the centre. Then use the tail centre of your lathe to mark the exact centre of the four segments on the cardboard.

Now use callipers to scratch circles onto the segments (Photo 3). Two rubber stops per segment require the additional lines (FIG 1)

Stops

A lot of different hard rubber stops, like door stops or even toilet seat stops, are offered by hardware stores. Chemical-supply shops sell softer tapered plugs of different sizes that work nicely. ▶

YOUR CHUCK

segments. For reasons that become clear later on, I chose a gap of 6mm ¼".

Marking out the gap is done by clamping a thin, straight piece of metal or wood between the wood jaw plates and putting a second straight piece against it to determine the position of the bandsaw –

Photo 2
Marking out the gap between the segments is done by clamping a thin, straight piece of metal or wood between the wood jaw plates and putting a second straight piece against it to determine the position of the bandsaw or scrollsaw cut.

Photo 3 Use callipers to scratch circles onto the segments.

FIG 1

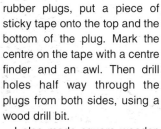

Holes to hold the frame for mounting heavy bowls

Segment

22.5°
45°
22.5°

Position of the holes for stops

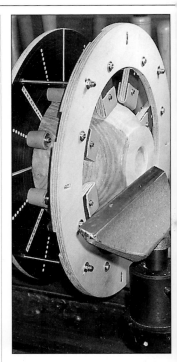

Photo 6
A wooden frame was made with eight adjustable tongues that can be used in combination with the chuck.

to turn holes into wooden discs by putting a round piece of scrapwood under the disc (see article about Candle UFOs in Issue 27 of *Woodturning*). Photo 5 shows the basic set. Note the extra long chuck key.

*M*ounting heavy and distorted bowls

When heavy bowls or bowls that have been pre-turned from green wood and distorted during the drying process need to be remounted on the lathe, an extra strong fixing is desirable.

I made a wooden frame with eight adjustable tongues that

If you need to drill holes into rubber plugs, put a piece of sticky tape onto the top and the bottom of the plug. Mark the centre on the tape with a centre finder and an awl. Then drill holes half way through the plugs from both sides, using a wood drill bit.

I also made square wooden stops to hold square workpieces (Photo 4). One of their faces is covered with rubber so they can be used with or without the rubber layer.

*F*urther applications

The chuck can also be used

Photo 5 The basic set. Note the extra long chuck key.

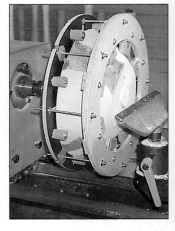

Photo 7
The slots between the segments can be used for fixing four additional threaded rods with extra big and strong homemade washers.

can be used in combination with the chuck described previously (Photo 6).

Four pieces of threaded rod fastened to the segments with nuts on both sides hold the frame in position. The fact that the holes in the segments travel according to how far the scroll chuck is opened, is compensated by slots I routed into the frame.

The slots between the segments can be used for fixing four additional threaded rods with extra big and strong homemade washers (this only works when there is a slot wide

enough to take the rods even when the chuck is fully closed). The washers also help to align the segments (Photo 7).

This frame could also be used with an ordinary big faceplate instead of the scroll chuck. In this case the convenience of centring and holding the workpiece with rubber

Photo 4 Wooden stops were made to hold square workpieces.

stops is lost, but this can be overcome by drawing circles onto the faceplate and using the tailstock for added support and safety.

Of course the frame can be used without the tongues if the size of the bowls you make doesn't vary much. I wanted a universal system without rings of different inner diameter, so I made three sets of wooden tongues.

Each size can be moved in a recess I routed into the frame and is held in position by bolts and wing nuts. The tips are rounded and leather-covered to protect the surface of the workpiece.

I chose 15mm ⅝" plywood for the 40mm 1 ⅝" wide tips.

The fact that the long tips flex slightly when the frame is tightened can be used to advantage when the workpiece is distorted and could be overcome by using thicker plywood.

For safety reasons, the tongues shouldn't protrude over the outer rim of the frame. Threaded rods of different

chose 15mm ⅝" plywood for the frame. Because the thickness depends on the diameter and the width of the frame you might want to vary it.

Now I transferred the drawing to the plywood board, drilled the holes and routed the slots and 4mm deep recesses that guide the tongues.

Next I cut around the outer diameter on the bandsaw and drilled a 2mm hole into the centre of the disc. I enlarged the surface of my faceplate with a particle board disc and turned it round.

Also, I drilled a 2mm hole

piece of the plywood disc and the later frame to the particular board disc, you can turn right through the plywood disc and round the edge in one go (Photos 9 and 10).

The tongues were numbered and drilled using the holes and recesses in the frame as a guide, because otherwise it is difficult get matching holes for the bolts that have to go through both pieces.

Mounting rectangular stock

You can modify the chuck-

Also, two straight adjustable jaws are bolted to the semicircles. (You need to do this first using bolts that have countersunk heads, when the bolts are positioned under the segment later on).

This economy version which saves the cost of a separate set of wood jaw plates has a slight drawback, because you cannot bolt the two pieces together where the wood jaw plates are.

Unfortunately, a lot of pressure is created in this place when the scroll chuck is tightened and the result is the two

Photos 9 and 10 When you fix the inner waste piece of the plywood disc and the later frame to the particle board disc you can turn right through the plywood disc and round the edge in one go.

plywood pieces try to bend away from each other.

This can partly be overcome by using thicker plywood than I did and by using turn buckles that create a counteracting force when tightened (Photo 11). Turn buckles have a right-

ing system for use on rectangular workpieces by bolting two semicircle-shaped plywood pieces to two segments opposite each other (FIG 2).

Photo 8 Threaded rods of different lengths complete the system.

lengths complete the system (Photo 8).

Making the frame

After making an actual size drawing on paper, I went through my wood bits and

into the centre of this disc, using a drill chuck held in the tailstock. A 2mm nail inserted through both holes helped to centre the plywood disc when it was screwed to the enlarged faceplate.

When you fix the inner waste

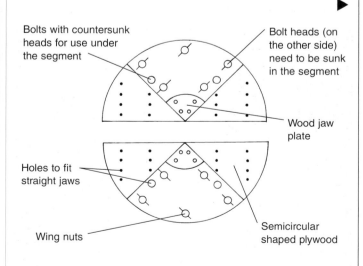

Bolts with countersunk heads for use under the segment

Bolt heads (on the other side) need to be sunk in the segment

Wood jaw plate

Holes to fit straight jaws

Wing nuts

Semicircular shaped plywood

FIG 2 Rear view

Photo 11 Turn buckles create a counteracting force when tightened.

Photo 12 When I tried to turn a spoon, my lathe taught me a lesson about centrifugal forces and unbalanced workpieces.

Photo 13 Additions to the chucking system

handed and a left-handed thread.

The combination of both creates an additional clamping force when they are turned in one direction and the pressure can be released by turning them into the other. They also serve as stops should a workpiece try to become airborne.

I used coachbolts to fix the turn buckles to the plywood. There needs to be some play between the bolts and the eyes of the turnbuckles.

Nuts that are countered (turned in opposite directions when tightened against each other) on the bolts act as spacers towards the wood surface.

Steps for mounting a workpiece

Take the following steps to mount a workpiece:

1 **Clamp** the workpiece with out the turnbuckles.
2 **Adjust** the distance between the bolts by turn ing the turnbuckle and insert the bolts through holes in the wood.
3 **Use** wing nuts to fasten the bolts.
4 **Turn** the turnbuckle to clamp the workpiece.

When I tried to turn a spoon, my lathe taught me a lesson about centrifugal forces and unbalanced workpieces. I remembered this funny looking German windmill that has only one blade and a weight to counterbalance it.

When I put a second wood-piece of exactly the same width into the chuck that filled the rest of the diameter, the problem was solved and my lathe stopped walking (Photo 12).

Photo 13 shows the additions to the chucking system and Photo 14 the complete system. ●

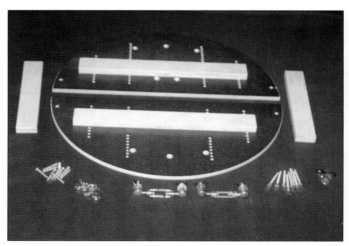

Photo 14 The complete system.

Safety

This chucking system might look a bit dangerous, but it can be operated safely when you are aware of possible safety risks and know how to handle them.

Be aware of protruding components of the chuck and keep your fingers behind the toolrest while the lathe is in operation.

Make sure all nuts and bolts are fastened securely and stop the lathe immediately you hear a suspicious sound.

Check the workpieces are fastened securely by trying to pull them out of the chuck before you start the lathe.

Use the tailstock for additional support when possible.

Start the lathe at a slow speed before you switch to higher speeds.

Don't stand in the firing line when you start the lathe and don't cross it while the lathe is running. I use a foot-operated remote switch for switching the lathe on and off when turning pieces which require extra caution.

EGGSACTLY

Here's an idea for a template from Ray Levy which will enable you to turn exact copies of wooden eggs, time after time.

Wanting to turn some wooden eggs, I looked through engineering handbooks for layout data. But a diligent search revealed nothing useful. Undaunted, I took the egg carton from the fridge and selected a well-shaped specimen.

I mounted this on a lump of putty and carefully traced its outline on paper. The tracing was enlarged to 255mm, 10" long and its profile faired smooth.

An accurately-drawn grid permitted coordinates to be taken off, resulting in the drawing shown here. All the numbers on it are multipliers and therefore non-dimensional. They'll apply equally well whether you work in inches, centimetres or cubits.

You need to know either the length or the diameter of your egg. Each number in the drawing has to be multiplied by the overall length, which will give you the dimension at that point.

If the limiting dimension is the diameter of your material, you can determine the length by dividing the radius of the stock by the largest radius multiplier, which is .320.

For example, a 75mm, 3" DIA blank has a radius of 38mm, 1 ½". Divide 1 ½ by .320 and you get 4.687, which is the overall length. Knowing this you can proceed with the layout.

Begin by drawing the horizontal datum line a little longer than required, and erect a perpendicular line near the left end. The intersection of these lines is the zero point and all lengths are measured from it to the right.

No errors

This eliminates any possible accumulation of errors. Multiply the overall length by each coordinate in turn and mark these distances from the zero point.

For example, a 125mm, 5" long egg would have verticals at 5 x .04 = .20, or 5 x .10 = .50, or 5 x .16 = .80 etc. Draw vertical lines at each point you have marked.

The profile points are measured up from the datum line. Multiply the overall length by the coordinate at each station. For example, 5 x .107 = .535, while 5 x .164 = .820, and 5 x .203 = 1.015, etc. This method is easiest to use with the metric system.

Use a draughtsman's curve to draw a fair line through all points. I glue these layouts to cardboard or thin plywood to make templates.

It's worthwhile making a second template of about ¾ length to use when the egg is still attached to the blank. I sometimes also make short templates for each end.

This procedure will allow you to turn eggs of uniform profile to any desired size. I hope you find it useful. ∎

Top: Hollow egg, maple, katalox and pernambuco, 100mm, 4" long, made by Ray Levy.

Offsets for eggs

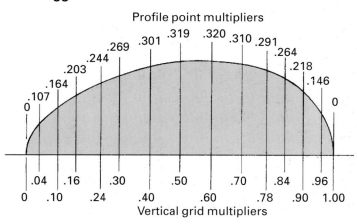

Profile point multipliers

.107 .164 .203 .244 .269 .301 .319 .320 .310 .291 .264 .218 .146
0   0

.04 .16 .30 .50 .70 .84 .96
0 .10 .24 .40 .60 .78 .90 1.00

Vertical grid multipliers

CHISEL CHANCE

Tony Evans, inventor of the 9-in-1 Multi Tool, tells how a lucky accident led to its invention

The 9-in-1 Multi Tool really invented itself. It began when I accidentally snapped off a 8mm, ⅜ in square beading chisel to an angle like that of the Multi Tool. I carelessly caught it on the jaws of a rotating chuck.

After finishing the workpiece with this broken chisel, which was still very sharp, I ground and honed it to the new angle – 45° on a single flat plane, diagonally corner to corner.

Having been a cabinet-maker with a lathe for many years, I knew a 'handy' chisel when I saw one. I also knew there were no woodturning chisels of this shape.

I called it my 'Splay' chisel, and found it had about nine uses.

About a year later, in a junk box of metal turning bits and pieces, I found a piece of diamond section high speed tool steel. It was 6mm, ¼ in across each flat and about 150mm, 6in long, in a junk box of metal turning bits and pieces.

I ground this diagonally too at 45° and fitted a handle. This, I found, was even more versatile than the square one. No matter what angle was offered to the

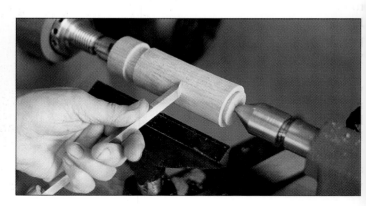

workpiece, it had a cutting edge.

It felt solid and comfortable to use, and did not easily 'dig in.' I now have a set of various sizes and lengths. The small ones, 5mm, 3⁄16 in, are little gems.

Some of the uses I've found for the Multi Tool are:

1 Neatly cutting V grooves of any size.
2 Undercutting beneath the top of a toadstool.
3 Boring into end grain and turning inside boxes and lids.
4 Rolling a bead, feeling easier and safer than a skew.
5 Cutting cleanly across end grain, right down to the steel lathe centres and shaping end corners.
6 Shear scraping efficiently on the outside of bowls or

cylinders with the tool pointing up or down. With the long point uppermost and clear of the rotation, it will plane easier than a skew and produce a superb finish.
7 Cutting dovetailed recesses or spigots to match the angles of chuck jaws.
8 Forming very fine detail.
9 Turning brass or copper tubing for tool handle ferrules, and for cleaning up the end of the ferrules to a safe-rounded corner.

A little practice is needed, as with all tools, to 'get the feel' of the various cutting angles.

I gave the tool deeper thought after colleagues had seen me use these tools, 'had a go,' then said they were an innovation which might even be termed an 'invention.

I decided to contact Craft

Scraping with the 9-in1. Even on an open grain, like oak, the finish is good.

Right: Shear scraping. The tip is well above centre, keeping the point clear of the wood.

The 9-in-1 Multi Tool, invented by Tony Evans and developed by Craft Supplies.

more uses than the nine I've suggested.

I feel humble and honoured to have contributed something to the world of woodturning so late in life. ∎

Supplies for advice and evaluation of my 'Splay' chisel's potential. I made an appointment with Nick Davidson in November 1995, driving through freezing fog to get there.

I explained the different uses to Nick and left two chisels with him for appraisal – a 'square' and a 'diamond.'

The rest, as they say, is history. Craft Supplies designed a combination of the two, half square, half diamond: the 9-in-1 Multi Tool was born.

A lot of interest

It is now manufactured by Craft Supplies and is creating a lot of interest in the woodturning world, receiving good reports wherever it goes.

The Multi Tool is simple to lightly grind and hone, having a single 45° flat plane. I don't recommend you hollow-grind it.

It may well be the only woodturning chisel which requires an 'operator's handbook' with all its known uses.

As its name suggests, it is a versatile tool, and other woodturners may find even

The edge on the left is cutting as a skew chisel. For a right cutting skew, swing the handle to the right.

Facing off using the long point. A dovetail spigot is formed at the same time.

The dovetail cutter version of the 9-in-1 is ground to a suitable angle for chuck recesses and spigots.

The author

Tony Evans, 65, is a fifth generation cabinetmaker, who started turning at the age of 11 on a home-made lathe.

He switched to the building trade in 1952, working in Africa and Iran, where he taught woodturning part-time.

He later settled in his home town of Chester.

After taking early retirement from Shell 10 years ago, Tony returned to cabinetmaking full-time.

He specialises in heavy woodturning, the one-ton crane above his 'no limit' lathe being proof of this.

Now enjoying an active semi-retirement with his wife Marie, they like gardening and travelling in their camper van.

In his spare time, when he isn't inventing chisels, Tony writes letters and articles for *Woodturning* magazine. He is also an active member of the Cheshire and North Wales Woodturners' Association.

It was an unusual commission to say the least – to turn wooden drum shells for an African music teacher.

Historically, the drums are carved from rainforest timber in the teacher, Tunde Solanke's Nigerian homeland. But after emigrating to Australia 15 years ago he finds the historic wood hard to get and says carving is too slow and expensive.

He has even resorted to having them made from terracota clay, which was acceptable musically, but a problem if you dropped one.

Tunde showed me a wooden drum which had been roughly hollowed with a chainsaw, and I felt the challenge to turn one take hold of me.

We discussed dimensions, construction and possible timbers. The shell was to be made in two parts, a top and a base. Before the two parts were glued, a metal ring had to be slipped over the base, to hold the skin's tensioning strings.

The drums which Australian emigrant David May was asked to turn were not only distant, originating in Nigeria, but were totally different from anything he had attempted before. He tells here how he went about it.

DIFFERENT

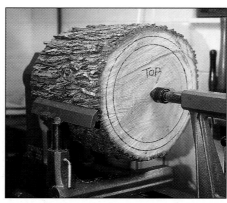

Above: The 40kg silky oak blank mounted between centres.

Roughing down with the 25mm, 1" Woodcut gouge.

The top rim diameter was to be 280mm, 11", 330mm, 13" or 380mm, 15".

My first consideration was to obtain suitable timber. The chainsaw drum Tunde had shown was only about 230mm, 9" DIA, but for the drum I was to make I'd need logs of at least 510mm, 20". It called for tree trunks rather than branches. And they had to be fresh-cut, as any seasoned or part-seasoned timber of that size would be cracked beyond use for musical instruments.

I felt reasonably confident that, provided the hollowing was done soon after the outside shaping, with a wall thickness of 13mm, ½", cracking during drying would not be a big problem.

Where I live, in South Queensland, four species of tree were suitable for

DRUMS

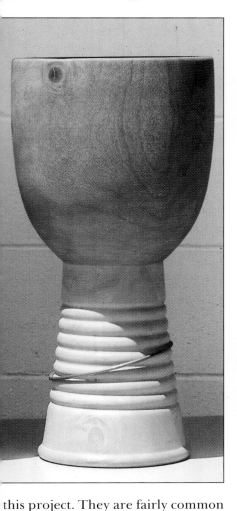

Left: Two finished drums, the one on the left skinned and ready to play.

Squaring the ends, the diameter at exactly 280mm, 11".

Hollowing the lower end of the top, between centres.

this project. They are fairly common in gardens and paddocks, but not often in the sizes I needed.

The four, camphor laurel (*Cinnamomium camphora*), jacaranda (*Jacaranda mimosaefolia*), silky oak (*Grevillea robusta*) and mango (*Mangifera indica*), are fast growing, light to medium-density timbers, fairly straight-grained with good colours.

I asked for help from friendly tree fellers and, within days, a log of silky oak appeared in my front garden – along with a large dent in the front lawn where it had been dumped from a truck. The log was 1.2m, 4 feet long and had a 460mm, 18" DIA.

A few days later, a pile of mango logs – none of which I could lift – were left piled in front of my garage. I had to chainsaw them before I could put the car away. They do have a dry sense of humour, these felling friends.

Now I had the timber, the next step was to get it on the lathe. I cut a 330mm, 13" length and marked and drilled accurate centres. It weighed over 40 kilos, 88lbs, so I needed help to mount it between centres.

Luckily, my lathe is Vicmarc's latest, a long bed version of the VL300, which has 1.2m 4 feet between centres and 600mm, about 24" DIA over the bed.

Exploring the limits

I love its variable speed. It has so much torque at minimum speed (190RPM) that it's unstoppable. I'm looking forward to exploring its limits.

I pressed the start button with trepidation. The log revolved quietly. There was some vibration, but not a lot. The 19mm, ¾" roughing gouge felt light and inadequate and I was uncomfortable with it.

Then I remembered a 25mm, 1" bowl-cum-roughing gouge given to me by Ken Port, of Woodcut Tools International (New Zealand), which I hadn't used on account of the weight. It has a solid 25mm, 1" shaft.

This was magic! The shavings flew across the workshop and the tool's weight meant there was virtually no vibration or kick from it.

Within minutes I had the bark and sapwood turned off and the log reduced to the required cylinder. I squared the ends to the correct length, then did the outside shaping.

My next problem was how to hollow the centre or, more importantly, how to mount it for hollowing.

For most hollow vessels made previously, I'd used a four-jaw scroll chuck, though they weren't this big. But I wanted to try it, and knew I could reverse ends on the work and maintain concentricity until I'd discovered the best method.

Because of the workpiece's weight, it had to be supported by the tailstock until the bulk of the hollowing was done. Before removing the work from between centres, I turned a 115mm, 4 ½" recess at the bottom end and a spigot of the same size at the top.

I fitted my big Vicmark VM140 chuck and used its incredible gripping power to hold the spigot. I set the speed to 300RPM. (Vicmarc have not fitted a tacho to these lathes yet, but I'm sure they will one day).

For hollowing end grain I have a selection of gouges, a long-handled version of the Mighty Midget, a House of Woodturning 25mm, 1" ring tool and a borrowed Sorby RS2000 kit. I tried them all.

Broke the tip

I soon found it was not going to be easy. But then, hollowing end grain never is! I broke off the tip of my Sorby RS2000 slicer by pushing it too hard.

The one that worked best was the Mighty Midget, with the gap set wide. I hung on to the long handle and let the shavings fly.

By hollowing the bottom first, with the tailstock in place and leaving a centre core, I reduced the wall to 25mm, 1" and about 100mm, 4" deep.

Then I reversed ends, mounting the base recess on the chuck in expansion mode. The chuck was now supporting what would be the outer shell and the tailstock supporting the core.

There was now more room for hollowing, and I could leave a 150mm, 6" core and 25mm, 1" wall thickness. I hollowed with the Mighty Midget to about 150mm, 6" deep and, with the tip of the Sorby slicer repaired, aimed for a break-through – a bit like the meeting in the Channel Tunnel.

I could hear the sound change as the thickness decreased until, suddenly, I broke through. The outer shell, sup-

ported by the chuck, kept turning, while the central core slumped and bounced a bit, held by the tailstock.

With the lathe stopped and headstock withdrawn, I extracted the core, which weighed 8 kilos, 19lbs.

I did the final shaping with the Mighty Midget and the ring tool, until I obtained an even 19mm, ¾" wall. Both tools left a crisp-cut finish which did not require further attention.

By now, the surface had dried a bit and could be sanded, followed by a coat of Penetrol oil and grain filler. This sealed the outer surface, so drying took place through the inner surface, which was less prone to split or crack.

Suppliers:

Woodcut Tools International,
PO Box 82, Morrinsville, New Zealand.
Tel or fax: 64-7-889 7757.

Vicmarc Machinery,
52, Grice Street, Clontarf, Queensland 4019, Australia.
Tel: 0061-7-3284-3103.
Fax: 0061-7-3283-4656.

Hollowing the top with the Mighty Midget, supported by chuck and tailstock.

The finished top shell weighed 5 kilos, 11 lbs. All that remained was to sweep up 27 kilos, 59 ½ lbs of shavings and to turn the base.

This was easier because it was lighter and smaller. I used camphor laurel, which is sweet to turn and has a strong aroma.

Tunde had given me the freedom to decorate it with beads, grooves, or whatever I fancied.

It was shaped in the same way as the top. The only difference was working space. But I overcame this limitation by making the centre core smaller and, when the weight was reduced, doing away with it and the tailstock.

I cut a spigot into the top of the base

The core removed. The chuck is just visible, expanded in the lower opening.

The completed base, hollowed in a similar way to the top.

Below: The two halves joined together are 560mm, 22" high.

to fit the recess in the upper half. If you make your own drum you will find that the joint remains acceptable if the two pieces are left joined during drying but before gluing.

If they are left apart and one piece is much drier than the other, they may never fit again. An alternative course is not to cut the spigot until after drying out. This is quite feasible, as the shells can be remounted on the chuck.

Whisked away

My first few drums were whisked away before the timber had a chance to dry. Indeed, the glue was still wet on one and the halves clamped together when it was collected, so I had no opportunity to see the effect of its drying out.

After obtaining a large log of silky oak, 600mm, about 24" in diameter, Tunde expressed an interest in 380mm, 15" and 405mm, 16" drums,

with a 16mm, ⅝" wall thickness.

I was able to hang on to these longer than the first ones, by the simple expedient of not telling him they were finished.

In Australia's sub-tropical climate of very low humidity, where the winter temperature can be 20DEG C, with high humidity and a nice warm 30DEG C in summer, you can almost see timber drying.

Some fine surface cracks developed, especially where any sap remained, but nothing serious. I remounted the half shells in the chuck and checked for distortion, but there were only minor changes, which couldn't be seen off the lathe.

Ironically, these two drums were the cause of the only complaint I have ever had, because silky oak is a very porous cellular timber which is quite light and did not produce the right tone for drums of this size.

Neverthless, I felt pleased with the drums I'd made, though I was put in my place at a Brisbane woodworking show. During the final packed hours of the show I saw two drums apparently floating through the crowd.

They belonged to John Allen, of Lismore in New South Wales, who, apparently, makes them in one piece, turning them on a huge lathe before kiln drying.

He then finishes the drums with skin, tensions the skins – and plays them! ■

The author

David May was born in Southampton in 1936 and his first brush with woodwork and woodturning was at Southampton Technical College.

At the age of 15 he joined the RAF as apprentice engine fitter and aircrew. He emigrated to Australia in 1964 and lives in Clontarf, Queensland. David retired in 1991, after 27 years as an air traffic controller.
He has been actively turning since 1982, and is a founder-member and past-president of the Redcliffe and District Woodcraft Society.
When he isn't woodturning, he enjoys boating, fishing and travelling.

Judith Parry, who took the photographs shown here and manipulated the word processor, also helped with some of the turning.

Getting the thread

American woodturner **Fred Holder** gives the amateur guide to hand chasing threads

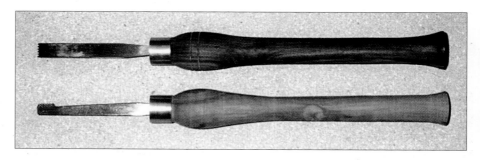

Thread chasing tools. The one for the outside thread (male) is on top

I had used taps and dies for more than 50 years, but had never heard of hand chasing threads until I read Bill Jones' column in *Woodturning*.

Once I knew of it, I found a section on screw cutting in *Hand or Simple Turning* by John Jacob Holtzapffel. The book devotes several pages to hand cutting threads with a chaser, but I didn't have one.

I read the instructions on how they were made, however, and tried to make my own (an outside chaser), but it didn't work. I blamed the chaser, along with my own lack of knowledge, but think the main problem was the wood was too soft.

About 18 months ago, I managed to buy some thread chasers from an English firm, G and M Tools, and began trying to make threads in wood.

Early efforts

My early efforts were poor to terrible, and unworkable with the lathe running. I tried apple, madrona, cherry, maple and several other local hardwoods without success.

Then I tried turning my Carba-Tec lathe by hand and began to obtain a fair thread in cocobolo and harder woods. Alternative ivory also threads beautifully with this method.

With a little practice I found I could make a functional thread in materials such as cocobolo, one of the iron-woods, plastic, and Dymondwood, which is a resin-impregnated coloured wood.

I've also been able to cut some nice ones in softer woods, such as apple, with the help of a little Hot Stuff (Red Label) cyanoacrylate adhesive.

Not difficult

It's not too difficult to do when you turn the lathe by hand, and a pair of thread chasers is less expensive than Bonnie Klein's attachment for the Klein lathe.

I'll talk about outside threads first, because they are easier to do, since you can see what is going on.

The first step is to turn a prepared blank to a diameter slightly bigger than the end product wanted. Give yourself some extra length, as the first thread or two will probably have to be cut away.

At the back of the area which is to be threaded, cut a recess – your stop thread area. This allows you to cut clean to the end of the threaded area.

Round over the end of the stock slightly to simplify starting the thread.

Fig 1 **The prepared male thread blank. Note the recess at the rear of the thread area.**

Fig 1 shows what the properly prepared blank should look like.

Place the toolrest parallel to the stock and grasp the chaser with your right hand, allowing the remainder of the handle to lie along your forearm for support.

With the chaser on the toolrest at a slight angle to the wood's axis (fig 2), start turning the lathe by hand. If ➤

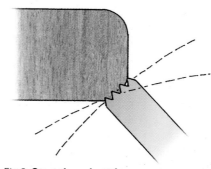

Fig 2 **Start thread cutting on the rounded over portion. Then straighten the tool so it can move along the part to be threaded.**

Cutting the male thread while turning the lathe with the handwheel.

➤ you don't have a lathe with a handwheel, you can make your own wheel and mount it between the faceplate and the spindle shoulder.

Amazingly, the tool crawls along the wood, scoring it lightly. Once it cuts into the recess, pull it away and return to the start.

Ensure you begin in the previously cut scoring or groove and begin turning the lathe again until the tool reaches the recess.

Repeat the process until the thread is fully cut and the outside diameter has reached its correct diameter.

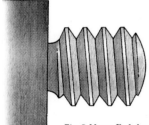

Fig 3 **Your finished male thread should look like this.**

If your thread is fully cut and the threaded piece still too big in diameter, use a square end tool to reduce it to near the proper diameter. Don't cut away so much that you eliminate your thread.

Now re-cut the thread until it is deep enough and you've reached the desired diameter. Fig 3 shows what your thread should look like.

Cutting the female thread is more difficult, but not as hard as getting it to fit the outside thread you've just cut. It's just that you can't properly see what you are doing.

Also, you are trying to get a specific size that will screw on to the male thread you've just cut, yet at the same time be not too loose.

The prepared blank is done in a similar same way to the male blank. Cut a hole in the stock a little smaller than the desired finished size (which should be a little larger than the diameter of the male screw measured at the bottom of the threads).

At the bottom of the hole, cut a recess as shown in fig 4. At the bottom of the hole, round the corner over slightly. Now you are ready to start thread chasing.

Fig 4 **The female threaded area should be the reverse of the male. Note the recess at the rear of the thread area.**

Place the T-rest at right angles to the axis of the hole and slightly below centre. Grasp the tool in the same way as for the male tool, letting the handle extend back along your forearm.

This time you have to be a bit more contorted, since the chaser's cutting edge must be about parallel with the surface of the hole.

Place the tool at a slight angle to the hole (fig 5) and start turning the lathe by hand. Again, magically, the tool begins crawling along the hole's surface. When it descends to the recess at the bottom of the hole, lift the tool from the wood.

Move back to the beginning, align with the shallow groove cut with the first pass, and repeat the process.

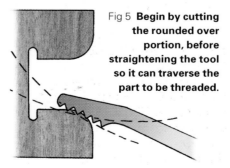

Fig 5 **Begin by cutting the rounded over portion, before straightening the tool so it can traverse the part to be threaded.**

Start with a simple nut and bolt.

Repeat until the thread is fully cut and/or the proper size has been reached. This is mainly trial and error.

Once the two pieces will screw together, I wax the threads to make the screwing easier. You may still have to touch-up one of the threads, however, to smooth their mating.

Don't rush to start cutting once they will screw together, or you could end up with a loose fit. Working them will polish the threads, and the wax helps smooth things.

Well, that's it! By the time you make half-a-gross, as Bill would say, you'll be a thread chaser. ∎

Suppliers

Hand chasers
G & M Tools ....Tel: 01903 892510
Tracy Tools Ltd.........Tel: 01803 833134

Alternative ivory
GPS Agencies ....Tel: 01243 574444

Alternative ivory and Dymondwood
John Boddy's Ltd.....Tel: 01423 322370
Craft Supplies ....Tel: 01298 871636

Timbers used

Apple *(Malus spp.)*
Cherry, American *(Prunus serotina)*
Cocobolo *(Dalbergia retusa)*
Madrona *(Ericaceae spp.)*
Maple *(Acer spp.)*

ADAPT A LATHE

Bertie Somme describes how he made his lathes more versatile, so opening the door to more turning opportunities.

The main drawback with any lathe is that it's limited as to what it can do. Sooner or later it won't be big, strong or versatile enough for the job in hand. There are two solutions – to buy a bigger lathe, or to adapt the one you've got.

Most of those mentioned here I've tried myself, others I've only heard about.

The Myford ML8 was my first serious lathe, and was king for adaptability. Its very strong headstock (with no swivel arrangement) is used by professional turners for really big items.

Slipping the belt

Peter Tree, of Lincolnshire, turned a 1535mm, 5' DIA tabletop on his lathe by adjusting the drivebelt tension so that the belt was slipping. By transmitting the power inefficiently the speed is reduced.

The necessary slippage for large items is easy to arrange on the ML8 because the hinged motor bracket is lockable in any position.

The headstock, of course, overhung the bench, and the turning called for the rash courage of the fanatical woodturner. For if the speed had built up too much, it would have been goodbye Peter. A 5', 1.5m DIA workpiece rotating at 200 RPM has a peripheral speed of about 36mph, 58kph.

Another of Peter's ideas is to use the end of a plank as a freestanding toolrest. One end of the plank is on the workshop floor, the other end is the toolrest. There is little bounce or give in a 'plankrest'. The only difficulty I have is in getting the height right on my lathe.

I've tried this and Peter's belt-slipping idea, and can vouch for them both. I'm reluctant to recommend others to follow our example on belt slipping due to the potential danger.

To make adaptations like these work, you need patience and understanding. You have to understand the principles of turning and have patience to devise and make the equipment properly.

It helps to look at things from upside down as well as sideways – inverted as well as lateral thinking.

Twists

For barleysugar twists, you need to lessen your lathe speed even more. Over 200 RPM simply won't work – about 20 RPM would be more like it. The treadle lathes used before the advent of electric ones, were ideal for this kind of work.

The Myford ML8 is also good for barleysugar twists, as it's easy to install a layshaft to add lower speeds. For those without an engineering back ground, a layshaft is an auxiliary drive shaft which enables extra speed ratios to be obtained.

In this case the layshaft is mounted on a hinged block above the motor. The motor is turned round so one belt runs from the motor to one end of the layshaft, another from the other end of the layshaft to the headstock. Each belt runs on a cluster of pulleys, giving me 16 speeds ranging from about 30 RPM up.

The block of wood the layshaft is mounted on is restrained by a leather strap, which has enough spring to allow the motor mount to provide the correct tension for both belts.

As turning techniques change according to whether you are using high or slow speeds, this adaptation opens the door to new shapes and possibilities.

Do remember to make some belt covers. Simple light boxes will do. You may not feel at risk from exposed

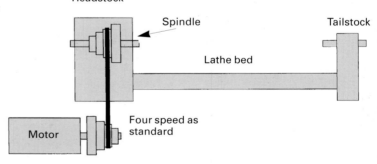

Standard drive belt arrangement. Not to scale

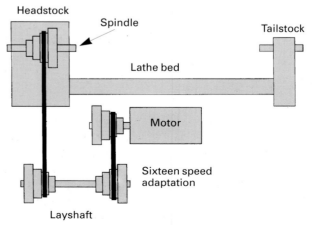

Adding layshaft to give greater speed range Not to scale

The Somme solution, a Graduate lathe with two bowl turning rests made of box section steel. The angle iron at the foot of the lathe gives additional floor fixings

A centre mark and concentric rings help position the wooden 'faceplate' on a rough turned bowl before fixing the metal faceplate.

drive belts, but can you be sure that a visitor won't accidentally get entangled and lose a finger?

My current lathe is a Harrison Graduate. It was a long bed version, but is now used exclusively in the bowl turning mode. It seemed a waste to have the long bed, which was fully equipped but remained idle because of a lack of toolrests.

I was also frustrated that the bowl turning outboard side of the machine only took 497mm, 19 ½" maximum diameter. What was I to do with planks

560mm, 22" wide – throw the excess away?

And when I did use it to full capacity, if the bowl warped badly, bits would have to be cut off so it could clear the lathe bed.

My adaptation to increase bowl turning capacity was constructed by an agricultural engineer, whose bill came to just over £100.

The top part of the two telescopic legs are made from 75mm, 3" box section steel. Inside each there is a threaded rod attached to the top of an interior section.

A handle on the top extends each leg to the floor. This gives a rigid toolrest and a brace for the rest of the machine.

Because I now have two toolrest positions, the inside and outside of the bowl can be turned without having to remount it. This suits me, as I finish the bottom of bowls by means other than turning.

This adaptation enables me to turn items of up to 1220mm, 48" DIA, if the floor will take it.

Floorbolts

The lathe is fastened to the floor by three floor-bolts inside and five outside. Four of the latter pass through the steel plate seen on the bottom right of the machine.

One of the nice things about this set up is that, when turning the inside of the bowl, you can always sit on the 'rest leg if you tire. Turning the outside of the bowl is the easiest part. I can even rest my elbow on top of the headstock.

A big problem when turning large pieces is balance. If big work is the slightest bit out of balance, even a lathe like this begins to rock.

Measures can be taken to correct this, such as the judicious use of a chainsaw to remove lumps from the heavy area. But when the piece is turned down to the level of the removal the problem may reoccur.

I've heard that the answer is lead weights but if one was to come loose, its trajectory would be 'interesting', even alarming.

My preferred method of attaching

bowls to the lathe is to use a steel faceplate, on to which is fixed a wooden faceplate which, in turn, is fixed to the bowl by dabs of hot melt glue. The bowl is removed either by a sharp blow or by wedges.

A pin in the centre of the faceplate is used to locate it centrally, aided by a series of concentric rings. I mark the centre and rings on the underside during rough turning. If I have to machine the base flat after drying, I make sure the centre mark survives so I can replace the rings.

The lathe I use most at present is an old Coronet Major. I've found few adaptations possible, though I have heard of someone who added some 20 extra feet on to the end of his.

I know Reg Sherwin had one with a 3050mm, 10' bed, so I guess there are possibilities. But the turning width is very limiting.

A major improvement I hope to make in future is to replace the lathe stand with two 45 gallon drums filled with concrete and sand. Sounds easy! ∎

The author

After attending a six-month Government Training Scheme, Bertie Somme worked for several large joinery firms and then a toy maker.
Following a few weeks roughing out for Richard Raffan, he started his own business, in 1979.
Bertie's training on both large and small woodworking machines, has led to a profusion of capabilities. His work ranges from chest of drawers to kitchen door knobs and salad bowls.
Bertie's main interest in woodturning is hand copyturning.

He describes his work as "heavy and staid", believing that the work is more important than the maker. Bertie runs weekend classes at his workshop in Tiverton, Devon.

STUCK ON

VIC WOOD

Dean Malcolm's first attempt at hot gluing a blank to a faceplate rather than using a chuck was on a small platter. Since then he has found the glue gun can effectively do the same for almost any piece of wood.

Photo 1 First, attach the bowl blank.

When Australian woodturner Dean Malcolm was looking to buy a chuck about 10 years ago, there were only a few available, and prices were high. Then someone mentioned hot glue.

Dean's first attempt at hot gluing was on a small platter and, to his surprise, it worked. He quickly found the glue gun could effectively hold most pieces of wood to a faceplate.

Wet or green wood was an exception. For big bowls, it was simply a case of providing a larger gluing surface.

To hold a block for a lidded box there was no need to rough a cylinder between centres and then chuck it. You just glued it to a block of wood, screwed it to a faceplate, waited a minute and started work.

The biggest advantage of hot glue is that it is strong yet can be cleaned off the surface without damaging the wood. This happens because, after applying the glue to one piece, the glue surface is allowed to cool a little before the two are brought together.

Another advantage is that you can cut right down to the glue join and even through it — no screws to worry about, so you can use every last bit of valuable timber.

With practice, almost any shape can be glued quickly and effectively. Importantly for Dean, hot glue allows for a flexibility in design not possible with other methods.

Here is a simple example of the hot glue method for turning a small bowl. First, attach the bowl blank with a screw centre, pin chuck or faceplate and screws (Photo 1). Or you can glue it to a scrap block.

Photo 2 Rough the back of the bowl to shape.

Rough the back of the bowl to shape, including the foot, then sand to 400 grit or finer (Photo 2).

If using Rustin's Danish oil, or any other finish, apply a coat and then burnish lightly on the base of the bowl before applying the glue (Photo 3).

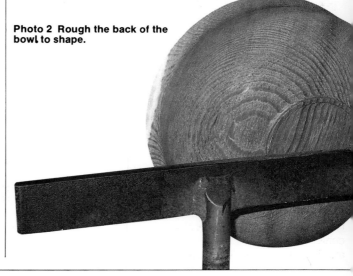

GLUE

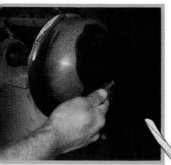

Photo 3 Apply a coat of finish.

> 'The biggest advantage of hot glue is that it is strong yet can be cleaned off the surface without damaging the wood.'

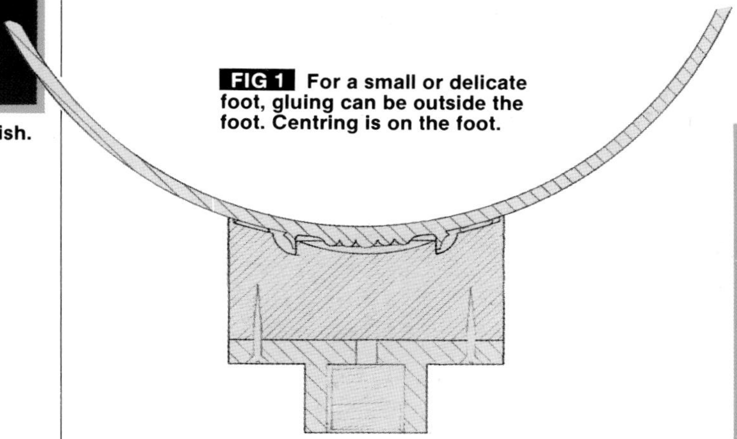

FIG 1 For a small or delicate foot, gluing can be outside the foot. Centring is on the foot.

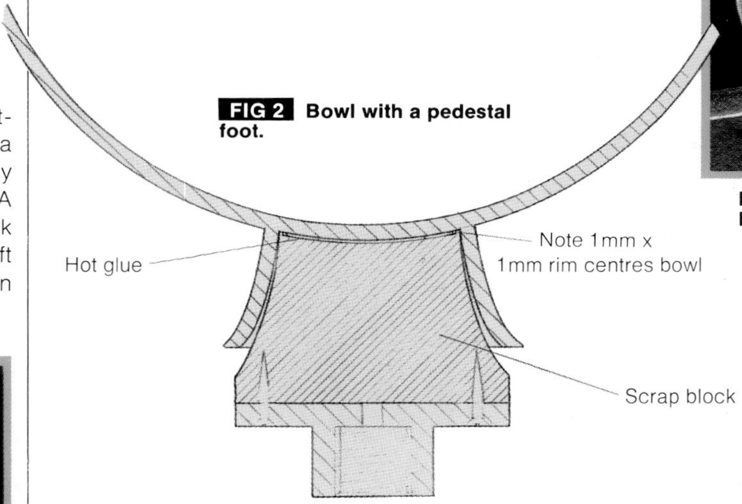

FIG 2 Bowl with a pedestal foot.

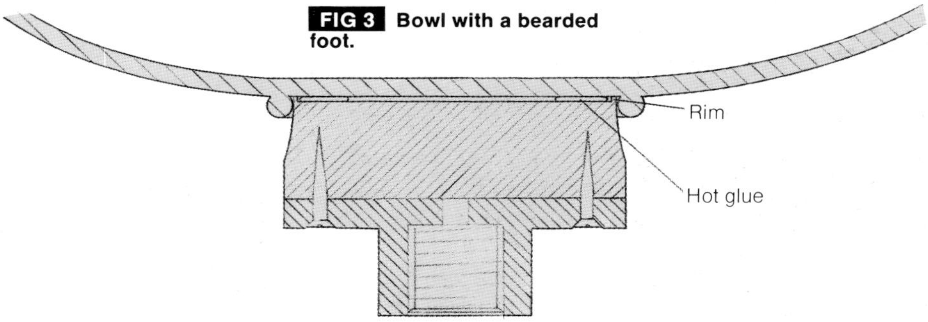

Hot glue

Note 1mm x 1mm rim centres bowl

Scrap block

FIG 3 Bowl with a bearded foot.

Rim

Hot glue

If you are not using a foot-ring (FIG 1) for centring, mark a pencil line just within any raised portion of the foot. A white pencil is helpful on dark wood (Photo 4), while a soft graphite, 2B or softer, is best on light timbers.

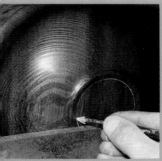

Photo 4 A white pencil is helpful on dark wood.

Remove the bowl from the faceplate and, using a screw centre or faceplate with screws, attach a small wooden block

similar in hardness to the timber used for the bowl (Photo 5).

Turn the block to just under the diameter of the circle drawn on the bowl base. On the bowl shown the circle was 63mm 2½" DIA and the scrap block was turned to 60mm 2⅜" DIA.

Turn a recess in the face of the scrap block some 1-1.5mm deep and to within 1mm of the edge. Place the scrap block on the base of the upturned bowl and check the alignment within the pencil line. ▶

Photo 5 Attach a small wooden block to the faceplate.

Apply hot glue to the scrap block (Photo 6). On cold days, warm the areas to be glued with a propane torch. This also applies to green timber. The beads of hot glue should sit above the rim level but not touch it (Photo 7).

At this stage it may be best to wait for a few seconds, allowing the surface of the glue to cool slightly, preventing it from sticking too firmly to the base of the bowl (Photo 8).

If you are unsure how well the glue will stick to your timber, experiment by gluing a

Photo 6 Apply hot glue to the scrap block.

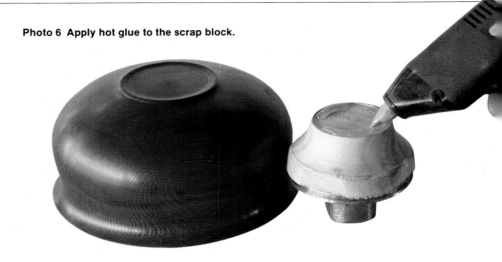

Photo 7 The beads of glue should sit above the rim level.

Photo 9 Align and press together.

Photo 8 Allow the surface to cool slightly.

Photo 10 Hollow the inside of the bowl.

piece to a bit of waste wood. Note the amount of glue you apply and the time between its application and bringing the surfaces together.

Allow two minutes to cool, then break the joint with a chisel. Vary the time and amount of glue until the join is strong but the glue remains on the scrap block and doesn't damage the other timber.

Experimentation over, press the scrap block attached to the faceplate to the bowl (Photo 9). Check the alignment and try not to move the joined pieces too much.

Clamping is not advisable. Allow the glue to set, usually about as long as it takes to sharpen a couple of tools.

Hollow the inside of the bowl (Photo 10). Dean uses a 12mm ½" bowl gouge. Sand and finish the inside of the bowl and complete all polishing, inside and out (Photo 11).

Standing behind the headstock, hold the rim of the bowl with your left hand and bump the back of the bowl with your right palm, as close as you can to the base (Photo 12).

The bowl should break free with a sharp crack as the glue gives way (Photo 13). If the bowl won't break off, part away a little of the scrap block next to the bowl's base and try again.

Sometimes a little glue will remain on the base (Photo 14). Do NOT use a chisel to remove it. Carefully pick the glue off with your fingers or dissolve with turps or lacquer thinner on a clean cloth (Photo 15).

Remove pencil lines with an eraser. Polish the base again by hand or you may like to remount on a vacuum plate.

The finished base should show no sign of how it was held (Photo 16). The completed bowl, mounted twice only, can be seen in Photos 17 and 18.

The scrap block can be used to hold another bowl — just turn the glue off with a gouge.

■

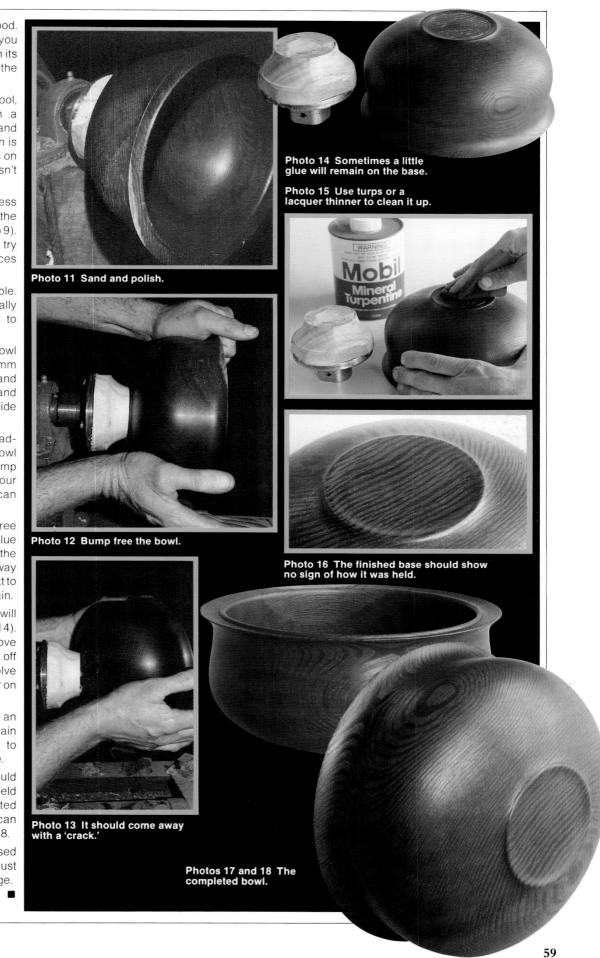

Photo 11 Sand and polish.

Photo 12 Bump free the bowl.

Photo 13 It should come away with a 'crack.'

Photo 14 Sometimes a little glue will remain on the base.

Photo 15 Use turps or a lacquer thinner to clean it up.

Photo 16 The finished base should show no sign of how it was held.

Photos 17 and 18 The completed bowl.

A QUESTION OF *style*

Maurice Mullins suggests ways in which turners can think laterally and so expand their horizons

Irregular burr oak platter, the inside dia 280mm, 11 in. It's not a piece for the faint-hearted, but experience breeds confidence.

Some two years ago I agreed to demonstrate at a creative woodturning seminar to be held at Horncastle Residential College in Lincolnshire.

I was to be in the illustrious company of Chris Stott and John Hunnex, both of them well known as creative woodturners.

But what could I, who had only demonstrated the techniques of turning and sharpening, possibly say about creativity.

It is, however, a subject close to my heart. I've had an art school training and gained an Open University credit in design products and processes.

The Open University made it clear to me that design is fundamental to success or failure. A woodturning is a product made from a specific process – it has to be turned. And at some stage the process also has to be designed.

House brick

At the seminar, students were split into three groups so each would have a session with each demonstrator.

I briefly outlined the importance of good design and then asked the students to tell me all the uses they could think of for a house brick.

At first, they seemed reluctant to enter into the spirit of the exercise. I could almost hearing them saying "What has this to do with woodturning?"

But they soon warmed up and came up with some brilliant suggestions. When it began to dawn on them that a brick is not just a brick, their boundaries of perception had been stretched a little.

▶

Peacock Platter, sycamore, 380mm, 15mm dia, with a 'Celtic' pattern and blue and gold inlaid rim.

Ovoid form, 130mm, 5 ⅛in high, made from wind-blown damson.

Using a traditional vase shape to experiment with ideas for boxes.

Later, a few students said they had wondered what I was trying to do to start with, but that it had eventually made them think. Yes, there's more ways than one to skin a cat!

And there's more ways than one to hollow a bowl! The above exercise in lateral thinking can help you work out problems in your own workshop.

The first thing to do is to identify the problem. A solution might not immediately appear, so try looking at the problem sideways.

As a short exercise, try the one I set the students? Give youself 10 minutes to think of as many uses as you can for a house brick.

Here are a few ideas to get you started:
- a hammer for nails;
- a sharpening stone for tools;
- a door stop;
- a wheel wedge for the car;
- a press for wild flowers;
- a block to raise your lathe.

Perhaps you can involve your family. Children are often better at it than adults. The older we get, the more constrained we become.

Now try the same with some other subjects, such as a car tyre, a skew, whatever... or how many different cuts you can make with a skew chisel? I'm a great believer in practice, as students of mine will know. I always advocate five or 10 minutes of warm-up work turning beads, hollows and cylinders, using wet or dry firewood.

It's an excellent way to get your hand and eye working together. You would not see Linford Christie sitting

Gallery bowl, walnut with yew beads, made from a plank 100mm, 4 in thick.

down to wait for the start of the 100-metres final. He'd be doing warm-up exercises and forming the right frame of mind, probably visualising himself leaving the rest of the field behind.

So give yourself five to 10 minutes practice before you start a piece, as it will give your work fluidity and assurance. Confidence is what you need – if you're timid in your work, it will show.

When to quit

How many times have you quit, knowing you should have done more, but afraid of making a mistake and spoiling the piece? I have, many times. Friends admire an item I have turned, but knowledge of its weaknesses haunt me. You can spoil something by not taking the risk and finishing it properly.

In my youth I was always asking the question, "How do they make that?" I do the same thing today. It's this enquiring nature – the dream of making something better by design – which has

The Three Graces, yew, 180mm, 7in high, with some hand carving.

Bowl in burr elm, 145mm, 5 ¾ in high, with a wall thickness of about 3mm, ⅛ in.

Platter in yew, 320mm, 12 ⁹⁄₁₆ in dia, its textured rim formed by turning on six different centres.

... led Mankind to develop the wheel and create the space shuttle.

Today, we can draw on all the woodturning knowledge there's ever been, from our local libraries. From that knowledge, I find the finished form is my priority. If I cannot make what is in my mind using the tools available, I make a new tool. Good turning! ■

The author

Maurice Mullins has always been a lover of wood. He was given his first semi-serious tool kit when he was four.

This attraction expanded at school, where his first encounter with the lathe was a little hairy.

Maurice explains how he ignored his teacher's instructions and increased the speed. A dig-in with the gouge sent one half of the six-inch candlestick he was making flying to the window.

The other half embedded itself in Maurice's cheek. He recalls "a lot of blood," but no stitches.

After recovering from the shock, the teacher gently persuaded him back to the lathe to complete the project. Maurice's mum still has the candlstick on display at home.

Many years passed before Maurice's next encounter with woodturning – on a private estate, where the maintenance manager had a workshop containing hundreds of tools.

Maurice would make some excuse to go there, and watched mesmerised as the chips flew.

He moved out of the area, to a house which had a small lean-to shed and, with the aid of some back-tax, bought an Arundel lathe from Alan Holtham.

It was a good starter lathe, having three speeds, with a cast-iron headstock and tailstock, each bored through with a No 1 Morse taper. Now he could start woodturning for real.

At the time, Maurice was working for himself felling and extracting softwoods from forestry land. It was strenuous work, to a point where his back began to complain.

Suddenly, he was off work for six months. He began to think about woodturning full-time, and began to read magazines and books on the subject, to visit shops, galleries, craft fairs and libraries. Maurice joined a six-week Start

Maurice Mullins in his workshop with one of his early solid Tall Vase forms.

Your Own Business course in Carlisle, to help him sort out a business plan and an accounting system. He decided his 'Unique Selling Point' was his design ability and training, which would enable him to produce quality, well designed work.

In September, 1983, he started turning full time. He had business cards printed which proudly announced, 'Maurice Mullins – Woodturner and Designer.' But although he was a designer by name, he had no formal design qualifications. A friend suggested an Open University course, which Maurice describes as "hard work, but brilliant." It enabled him to see his work – and others – in a new light.

He obtained a Northern Arts grant to buy a better, more substantial lathe and began turning items for craft shows, shops and trade shows and exhibitions.

The ball "was now being pushed up the hill towards that elusive pot of gold." The trouble is, just as he is nearly within reach, he says something happens to bring him tumbling down again.

Maurice Mullins,
Whelpo Farm, Caldbeck,
Wigton, Carlisle, Cumbria CA7 8HQ

Design in brief

Mention the word 'Design' to woodturners and they look as if the conversation has gone over their heads. Phrases such as "I can't draw", or "arty turning" come into play.

In my previous article on design (see page 60), I described an exercise to stimulate lateral thinking, to improve your turnings. In this article I'll tell you more design techniques to better your approach to work.

But first, "What is design, and what can it do for me or for you?" There are thousands of definitions, but mine goes like this:

"Design is a directed problem-solving process that can be applied to anything man made."

Now it's your turn! Jot down what 'design' means to you, and how it can improve your work. Many woodturning hobbyists dream of owning a well-equipped workshop and maybe earning enough to survive on by turning full or part-time.

Not easy

But it's not as easy as you might think! At the end of the day, the quality and design of your work will reflect how the public will view it and whether they will support you with sales. The standard of work is improving all the time. You only have to attend AWGB seminars to see that. Whether the work is a bowl, spindle, or sculpted piece, black, white or rainbow coloured, waxed, textured or raw, the public is becoming more interested and aware of quality.

Now for another exercise. Don't read any further unless you have 10 minutes to spare.

Take an A4 sheet of paper from your file or sketch pad and design a chair. You have 10 minutes to do it.

Right, that's it – your 10 minutes are up. Has the exercise borne fruit? Some of you might have drawn the chair you are sitting on. Clever! It's one answer, after all.

But you should have asked the following questions:

What will the chair be made from – plywood, PVC, stone, brick, wood, metal, or glass?

Maurice Mullins continues his series on design by stressing the need to sketch potential shapes and to set yourself a 'brief' before you start turning

Embryo Bowl, **made from one piece of 300-year-old elm**.

How high should it be – to suit a baby, a child, or an adult?

Is it to be a permanent fixture – to be placed in some public place, for example? Will it be stackable – school chairs etc.

As you can see, the exercise was more or less a failure because you did not have an adequate brief to work from.

What is a brief? Well, it is detailed information given to a designer, who uses his or her creative techniques to solve a stated problem. If you just grab a piece of wood, put it on the lathe and think, "What can I make out of this?" you will sometimes obtain a satisfactory result – but your success rate will not be good. I know, because I've done it myself.

It's fun to proudly show something saved from becoming an offering to the god of fire, but better to be positive in your approach.

Before you start work on a piece, clearly state what you want to make, it's shape and size, and what material you will use.

As the photos show, most of this information can be quickly and easily

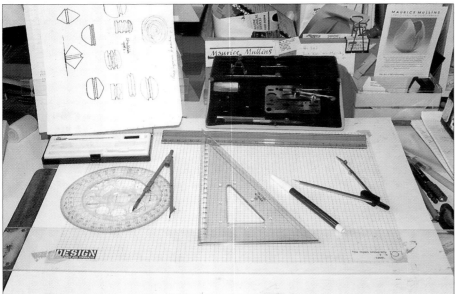

A traditional drawing board, made from Conti-board, and a home-made tee-square.

The quality and design of your work will determine whether the public will buy it.

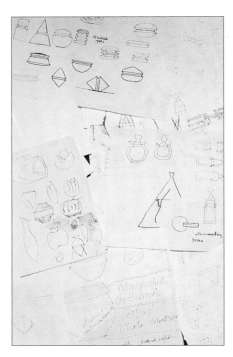

Some of the author's sketches. They do not need to be works of art.

worked out from sketches drawn onto paper.

You could even turn a piece of scrapwood into the shape drawn, so you can see it in three dimensions. If I want to change the shape of, say, a goblet, I first turn one from scrapwood.

All I'm interested in is its form, not finish, size or cost. I then have a useful model to help me decide whether I have solved my 'brief.'

As a process engineer, I was always amazed at the importance of a sketch. It enabled most problems to be seen in a fresh light. ➤

More items designed and turned by Maurice Mullins.

➤ The initial sketch was often drawn on a scrap of paper and would win no prizes in a drawing competition. But it didn't matter – the sketch was simply a means to an end.

Sooner or later, your brain reaches overload. A quick sketch puts on paper what has been achieved so far. It's a solution to a problem.

Why not photograph your work at various stages. This will enable you to see how far you've progressed towards solving a problem. If you are happy with your solution, move to the lathe. If not, return to the drawing board.

I recall a meeting of the Cumbria Woodturners' Association at Tony Caplin's workshop. Guest presenter was Merryll Saylan, who was demonstrating the use of colour and texture to enhance form. At one point, Merryll asked, "How many of you use a sketch book?"

After a pause, I put my hand up. Only three or four others, out of 35 people, did the same.

I have sketched and doodled from an early age, so never considered whether or not a sketch would benefit the result I sought.

I make sketches before selecting suitable wood or setting up the lathe. After drawing a piece I like, I make another sketch to add detail. This practice has saved me hours of trying to remember how I did something in the first place.

We process engineers would have brainstorming sessions to solve difficult problems which did not respond to normal methods and experiences.

Brainstorming is a quick-fire way of bringing to mind anything connected with a problem and jotting it down. Your minds run riot, generating ideas. It's a technique which can be done on your own, but it's even more efficient if two or more heads can get together, sparking ideas from one another.

I hope it's becoming clear to you that a pencil and paper, and perhaps a small A3 size drawing board, will dramatically improve your designs.

It will do more for you than the most expensive chuck you can buy, at a fraction of the cost. Give it a go – you have nothing to lose and much to gain! ■

Computers can be fickle. Pencil and paper can still compete on cost, convenience and ease of use.

The author

Maurice Mullins started turning full-time in 1983, and his business cards proudly announced 'Woodturner and Designer.' But he had no formal design qualifications. An Open University course changed all that, and enabled him to see his work – and others – in a new light. He lives and runs woodturning courses at Whelpo Farm, Caldbeck, Wigton, Cumbria.

R. J. Emery's career started in engineering on the shop floor at CAV Acton in the mid-30s. As it was the thing in those days to 'better oneself', he moved from job to job in fairly rapid succession. Not only was practical engineering encompassed but also the technical aspect and some office work.

During the latter part of the war in REME, he was seconded to a branch of the ISRB, working in the Design Office on various 'interesting' projects.

A brief spell in Canada followed in 1947 — on glassware mould design. Back home, he worked in the DO of a rubber manufacturer, also on mould design. His last job, as an employee, was as an assistant works manager in the early days of plastics, in Hertfordshire where he has lived for the past 40 years.

Rude words with (and to!) the manager, led to RJE starting a freelance engineering/ product design and modelmaking service . . . from one of the bedrooms.

That progressed from scratching a living (it was the 50s, not the 80s!) for the first few years, to building a small family business, ably partnered by his wife, which is now run by their two sons.

The making of 'Archifacts' and the engineering associated with them provide an active retirement.

ARCHIFACTS BY LATHE AND MILL

R. J. EMERY

The first of a two-part article in which the author, a miller turned turner, describes the techniques he uses to produce decorative pieces with a difference on an engineer's lathe.

Part 1: Mainly the Process

1. The well-used 'Omnimill'

Over the years I have set myself up with a goodly assortment of engineers' tools, including a lathe and a small milling machine. The restoration of a 1934 Talbot occupied much of my time for 8 happy years . . . towards the end of which I retired and soon found myself at a loose end.

Looking for something to fill the void, I happened across a woodworking journal and discovered the 'wonderful world of woods'. I also noticed mention of ornamental lathes and the 'barley stick' forms which they could produce.

Contemplating the 'barley' legs on our hall table one day, it struck me that if the helices were of a gentler angle, a greater degree of elegance would result — especially if combined with other than cylindrical forms.

I felt that what was needed was a means whereby a turned cylindrical, or other form, could be rotated slowly, by hand wheel, between centres in the horizontal plane as on a lathe. So slowly, in fact, that the form would make just one rev for about 200 revs of the hand wheel.

Also needed would be a table which has horizontal (xx & yy) and vertical movements, on which the centres can be mounted and, to complete the requirements, vertical cutting facilities with rise and fall motions . . . in other words, a vertical milling machine.

My small, well-used 'Omnimill' is shown in Photo 1.

After some tentative forays, I started producing 'decorative' pieces in both exotic and home-grown woods — turning the main form and applying the 'decoration' on the mill with suitable reduction gearing attached. That was some $2\frac{1}{2}$ years ago so that really, I am only a novice at woodwork.

Archimedes

Essentially I am a machinist; most, but not all, of the pieces embody a variation of the helical form and as my humble tribute to Archimedes, who is generally credited with being the originator of the screw/spiral form, I call them 'Archi-facts'. A selection is shown in Photos 2, 3 and 4.

2. Imbuya 63mm 2½" dia x 290mm 11½" tall →

3. Rosewood with Box inserts. 50mm 2" dia x 300mm 11¾" tall → →

4. Spanish Olive. 235mm 9¼" tall → → →

To the engineers among wood-workers, the system I use is wholly logical. As can be seen from Photo 5, part of the set-up comprises a pair of standard cast iron angle brackets (which are obtainable either partially or fully machined) which have been bored in line to take made-up centres and machined to fit the T-bolt slots and to take clamping bolts. The left hand 'centre' is an important item and is, in fact a 12mm ½" diameter silver steel 'stub axle' about 95mm 3¾" long, machined at one end to a cruciform.

5. A view of the set-up

This axle also has a flat for an Allen screw to lock it to a made-up dividing plate. The latter is spigotted on to a 'drive-drum', with a close revolving fit, which has four 6mm ¼" BSF tapped holes coinciding radially with the PCD of those in the dividing plate. The tapped

holes are for a conical registering screw which I have found preferable to any form of spring-loaded registering device — for reasons which I will touch on later.

Assuming that the wood is square to start with, it is centre-drilled at each end and band sawn to an octagon, see Photo 6. Then, set up in the four jaw (or using a drive centre), the other end is held by the tailstock centre and 50mm

6. From round . . . to square . . . to octagonal . . . to round!

2" or 75mm 3" of length is turned to dispose of the flats. That end is now held in the three jaw and the tailstock end also turned to allow support by a fixed three way steady.

The 12mm ½" hole can now be drilled some 50mm 2" deep and the axle pushed into it by the tailstock and then lightly driven in to ensure a firm grip in the base of the hole. I keep a newish 12mm ½" drill aside for that job, with an acute angled point to ensure a good grip for the cruciform flukes. I have even used a hand reamer in the tailstock to achieve a good fitting hole.

The axle also acts as an excellent means of holding the product in the vice for hand finishing — keeping the product well clear of damage from 'Jaws'.

It is worth mentioning, at this early stage, that if the wood is suspected of being damp, a smear of light grease or a touch of WD40 to the cruciform end of the stub axle will help in both inserting and more important, when removing it after final finishing. The stub must be drawn out axially until the flukes are clear and if it is rusted in, the knocking / levering out process can so easily damage a nicely finished piece — to say nothing of the moisture pitting the axle itself.

Thus far, I have described the components which comprise the product mounting system and before going on to outline the rotating system, it might provide interest to mention an earlier set-up I tried — which was my original conception and which I now feel is something of a joke!

Reference to Photos 7 and 8 will show that basically the system sets out to demonstrate that, if one end of a rod slides along an angled shaft at right angles to it and the other end of the rod slides tangentially along the periphery of the drive-drum, itself also at right angles to it, a degree of rotary motion of the latter is achieved. Note white 'quadrant' of rotation.

It did work! . . . but I decided that the resulting slow helices were not acceptable and that the whole set-up in its present form was too flimsy to overcome the frictions involved and to offer smooth operation. Nevertheless, it did provide a lot of interesting engineering.

Alternatives appeared to be either racking attached to the stationary part of the machine at the back of the table with a series of pinions, bevels and shafts hooked up to the drive-drum, or some sort of gearing attached to the table lead screw shaft.

Worm and Wheel

It was then that I came across a pair of worm and wheel gearboxes, long since 'lost' in one of the boxes of 'Os and Ss'. These units were made by Bonds o' Euston Road. Regrettably, they are no longer available from Bonds (although a good range of works and wheels is featured in their current catalogue), for they are of robust construction, with 12mm ½" diameter shafts and are well suited to the job in hand.

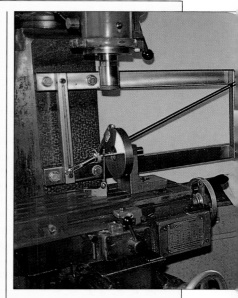

7/8. Note 'white quadrant' of rotation

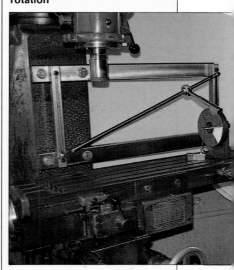

The ratios of these boxes were 10:1 and 30:1, so that connecting the output (wheel) shaft of the former to the input (work) shaft of the latter, gave a final drive of 300:1. In experimenting with pencil lines on plain cylinders, however, the resulting helix again seemed to be *too* gentle. Replacement ratios of 12:1 and 16:1 gave a final drive of 192:1 which seemed to be

---

Contemplating the 'barley' legs on our hall table one day, it struck me that if the helices were of a gentler angle, a greater degree of elegance would result — especially if combined with other than cylindrical forms.

---

about right and offered an acceptable degree of helix on both short and long products.

Photos 9 and 10 show the sub-assembly, with the essential in-line, albeit off-set, shaft layout, mounted on a channel section machined to line up accurately with the centre of the drive drum when bolted to the mill table. The final drive wheel shaft is a push fit into a shaft protruding from the drive drum and grub screwed in place.

The latter shot also shows a nest of tuned ali. pulleys fitted to the 10:1 gear box input shaft which is supported by an out-rigged brass support plate with a nylon bush. Very conveniently, the left hand end of the table screw has a plain portion of shaft protruding some 75mm 3" and fitted with a sleeve for adjustment purposes. This sleeve was replaced by a matching nest of pulleys keyed to the shaft.

The pulley grooves are machined to suit standard 6mm 1/4" diameter polyurethane

9/10. The sub-assembly

round belting which can be cut and 'welded' (with a hot knife) to suit the required tension. This belting, incidentally, is very efficient and the weld really does hold against quite high loads. However, the belt does need to be taut and it and the sheaves kept free from grease to prevent belt slack and slip — and hence belt vibration. I keep a second, slightly longer belt which, when twisted, reverses the direction of drive and helix.

Achilles' Heel

The mechanical 'Achilles' Heel' of this set-up is the backlash in the gear boxes — creating unwanted vibration when taking side cuts on the product. This shows up as a gap of some 60 thou. between lines scribed on the periphery of the 125mm 5" diameter drive-drum at the two extremities of the backlash. Hence the angled bracket, drilled for T-bolt holes and yoked at the outer end to take a nylon (or w h y) pulley. The cord is attached to the drive drum at one end and to a 10lb weight at

the other. Generally, it is very effective — merely needing a little hand assistance from time to time when the other hand is too heavy!

As touched on earlier, it was the 'barley stick' type of helix form which triggered things off. I realised that there was a specific technique involved in producing such forms, but at that time I knew nothing more beyond having seen diminutive illustrations accompanying ads for a lathe apparently designed for the purpose.

I have recently perused Mr T. D. Walshaw's book 'Ornamental Turning'; what a world of engineering complexity and ingenuity he writes about in such detail! I am duly impressed, out-classed and somewhat chastened . . . and I'm sticking to my simple 'Archifacts'!

Proportion

Having also been involved in product design over the years, I am conscious of what is probably the one, single, element which makes or mars a given design — namely, proportion. I have no artistic talent — I am in awe and admiration of some of the numerous sculptors and carvers featured in the wood-working journals — and so I have to fall back on the engineering adage: *'If it looks right, then usually it is right!'*

I had immersed myself in woodworking journals and catalogues and invested in *World Woods in Colour* which is very informative . . . but you can't beat going to the suppliers to see and feel the various woods available. I was absolutely enchanted by some of the home grown and exotic woods on show . . . mostly bowls, it seemed! I wondered about the mass of conflicting verbiage being put out on reafforestation and management but I respect and support the conservation aims involved.

I bought 'dry' wood, usually something in the order of 63mm/75mm 2½"/3" sqr. x

305mm 12". Later, I found a source of up to 125mm 5" sqr. x 460mm 18". It always bemuses me to think that trees grow in round form. I buy wood which has been cut into squares . . . all ready for me to turn into round form!

I have made 23 'Archifacts' since November 1988 — the first few as Christmas presents for the family and friends. There were also numerous 'trials and errors' — mostly errors (see Photo 11) but in the process I did prove that the machining system was effective and consistently accurate and I learned how mad I could (or could not) go with which cutters on which wood.

11. 'Trials and errors'

Cocobolo

Without doubt the best wood for machining I have found so far is Cocobolo followed closely by Kingswood. The former turns like a piece of free cutting brass and almost polishes likewise. A few others I have used are Imbuya, Tulip, Spanish Olive, various Rosewoods, Yew, She Oak and Purple Heart, plus Pear and Laburnum from our own garden.

Each wood has its own characteristics and it is interesting to note the difference there can be between turning and milling the same piece. I have often achieved a first class, almost polish, finish by turning off a few thou. with diamond lapped tool and then had a 'rough time' with it on the mill — irrespective of whether the piece was being grooved or side cut and of the direction of cutter travel.

In the second part of this article, which follows, the author describes the machining methods he uses to produce various types of wooden 'Archifacts'. ■

R. J. Emery's career started in engineering on the shop floor at CAV Acton in the mid-30s. As it was the thing in those days to 'better oneself', he moved from job to job in fairly rapid succession. Not only was practical engineering encompassed but also the technical aspect and some office work.

During the latter part of the war in REME, he was seconded to a branch of the ISRB, working in the Design Office on various 'interesting' projects.

A brief spell in Canada followed in 1947 — on glassware mould design. Back home, he worked in the DO of a rubber manufacturer, also on mould design. His last job, as an employee, was as an assistant works manager in the early days of plastics, in Hertfordshire where he has lived for the past 40 years.

Rude words with (and to!) the manager, led to RJE starting a freelance engineering/ product design and modelmaking service . . . from one of the bedrooms.

That progressed from scratching a living (it was the 50s, not the 80s!) for the first few years, to building a small family business, ably partnered by his wife, which is now run by their two sons.

The making of 'Archifacts' and the engineering associated with them provide an active retirement.

MORE ABOUT ARCHIFACTS AND THE PROCESS

R. J. EMERY

The concluding part of an article describing the techniques which the author, a miller turned turner, uses to produce decorative pieces with a difference on an engineer's lathe.

Part 2: The Machining Methods

Gradually I learned the technique/art of getting a fine finish on the various woods. I was determined from the start not to use any staining or colouring — the shades, texture and graining of the wood itself would have to stand by their own virtue . . . I would just assist with finishing, the sanding-sealer and waxing.

Usually I draw up the outline of the product with overall sizes and radii as a guide only — for acceptable proportions on paper may not be so in 'the wood'. Also, allowances for cleaning up one end for it to stand on, and for removing the centre drill hole from the other end, are best made on the drawing.

When rough turning a piece which is tapered at both ends, I remove much of the wood by putting the saddle on slow auto. feed while feeding the cross slide in and out by hand as necessary — a trick which is not recommended on materials other than wood! The form is then finished by hand turning — or scraping, as I have seen it described — to a template made from the drawing.

The importance of top quality machine and hand lathe work at this stage cannot be over stressed. Any eccentricity will become only too apparent when milling multi flats, flutes or other features where narrow 'lands' remain — e.g. Photo 2. This point is touched on again later.

Exercise

The product is now ready to go up on the mill so let us follow the progress of a simple example, similar to that shown in Photo 12. It is an exercise, in soft wood, featuring parallel 'flats on the twist', leaving

Photo 12

about 20mm ³⁄₄″ of body and with radii near the base larger than the 'flatting' cutter would leave. A pencil stub held in the m/c chuck, impinging lightly on the wood and the table, wound along, will mark out the lines to be worked to — see Photo 13.

Photo 13

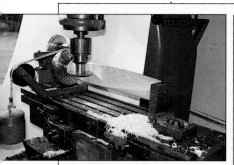

Photo 14

I have found that standard engineering cutters (provided they are sharp) are perfectly satisfactory with the 3,600 max. revs. on the mill. In any event, I find that smoothing out minor cutter marks is part of the pleasurable hand finishing process. The cutter shown in Photo 14 is a 20mm ¾" ø, long series end mill which makes short work of producing the flats. It is fed along steadily, one side at a time, towards the 'drive' end, in a series of cuts of about 3mm ⅛" until just a finishing cut is left. It is stopped short of the end by the amount of plain cylinder to be left, plus 50mm 2".

Now comes into play another cutter which I have used extensively — namely a 75mm 3" ø x 3mm ⅛" slitting saw. The one shown in Photo 14 has radiused teeth but the standard square teeth work quite satisfactorily, needing just a little more care. Up and down cuts of 25 to 30 thou., depending on the wood, can be made, reducing on approaching the finishing cut. The product is fed towards the saw, gradually in alternate xx and yy directions, so that the cutter just kisses the pencil line and leaving the desired length of base diameter. At that stage, the table stop is set to establish the cutter-centre position.

A point to mention here: **it is important that the table feed, especially when approaching the finishing cut, is always in the same direction** — preferably feeding against the rotation of the cutter, although that is not vital if a touch of lock is put on the table. **Cutting when returning the table is**

fatal; the product is contra-rotated by the back-lash in the gearing and the cutter impinges on the previous cut . . . and rude words could be uttered!

The first flat can now be machined to size with the end mill coming up to the table stop . . . but careful! Although both cutter centres will stop at the same place — and theoretically, both cuts should coincide — practice doesn't prove the theory. It can be explained by the difference between the diameters and travel of the two cutters; the saw travels vertically with the product remaining stationary while the end mill travels horizontally and the product continues to rotate on its helical path right up until the last . . . so that there is always a little to take out by hand — carefully! It is always preferable, for obvious reasons, to cut the flat-width in one go, so the cutter flute-length needs to be adequate.

As mentioned before, vibration plays its part in these machining operations. This applies especially when cutting the

Photo 16

second flat — when the wood is getting a trifle slim; hence the earlier remarks on using a conical screw to positively lock the dividing plate and the necessity for a slip and slack-free belt drive.

The slitting saw previously referred to has also been used to produce the various top-end features on several of the pieces to add to the general interest. These operations are carried out by holding the product in a split wooden collar, suitably formed and lined to protect the finish, which in turn is held in the machine vice. That allows the product to be revolved on its own axis and the vice to be swivelled to present a variety of compound angles to the cutter — see Photo 15. Care must be taken here to ensure that the

Photo 17

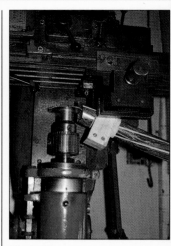

Photo 15

saw is cutting 'with' the fibres and that they are severed cleanly and not fractured. Needless to say, the saw needs to be sharp.

Photo 19

Photo 20

While much of the making of 'Archifacts' is carried out on the mill, preparatory and finishing work on the lathe, as outlined, is all important. Endeavouring to fine-finish by hand original turned surfaces left after milling, with the resulting loss of crisp edges, etc., is not recommended.

Further examples of 'side-cut' 'Archifacts' are shown in Photo 16. The square and triangular forms, in English Yew, both machined from cylinders, of course, have 45mm 1¾" and 50mm 2" flats respectively . . . no, the latter is NOT 'drunk' — but viewed from

Photo 20A

any angle it certainly does appear so!

More Complex

Moving on now to something a little more complex, Photo 17 shows an 'Archifact', in Pernambuco, 50mm 2" ø at the base x 310mm 12¼" tall. It is very satisfying to work with and

takes quite a good finish. I had always wanted to make a piece which shows what the 'inside' of the wood looks like and I made several trial runs in soft wood to prove the principle.

For this exercise, I made up a special cutter (shown in Photo 18) a piece of ⅛" gauge plate with the two main radii ground on opposing edges on a jig and the end rad. hand ground and stoned. After hardening and tempering, it was fitted to a split arbor and used virtually as a finishing cutter after the majority of the wood had been taken away by a series of end mills.

It will be apparent from this piece that another function is needed, in addition to the two normal vertical and horizontal movements of the machine, in order to produce the gradual run-out at each end of the fluting. This highlights one of the limitations of the milling machine — the inherent inability of any of its movements to follow a curved path . . . but then, the same applies to the lathe. If one wishes to follow a contour, one has to fit a copying attachment; and so with the mill — except that, the quill is not restricted by a lead screw — merely operated by a sprung hand lever as on a drilling machine.

Photo 18 ✏ **Photo 18A**

Contours

There is a natural elegance about the tapered ends of a flute made by a ball nose cutter slicing through a barrel form in a straight, (or helical) level line. That elegance can be simulated on cylindrical pieces and Photo 18A shows that 6mm ¼" thick Perspex makes an ideal template for producing tapers and contours. Clamped to the angle plate (which allows for ease of adjustment) it provides a smooth, hard surface for the ball-race follower.

The best method I have found of cutting these contours smoothly, especially when nearing the finishing cuts, is by travelling 'down hill' on the template. While that is satisfactory at one end of the product, in order to maintain the desired same direction of cutter-travel, 'up hill' cutting is inevitable at the other end . . . but judicious finger tip control of the quill lever will ensure good results.

It cannot be seen in Photo 17 but the tip of this 'Archifact' is not the original; when finishing off that end, a deep split appeared. Sooner than spoil the proportions, a piece was let in — not very handsome, but it was all hand work . . . and it **is** from the same piece of wood. A

small compensation was, when mounting the finished product in the lathe with a false end for the tailstock centre and spinning it freely, the 'internal' points formed by the meeting of the three flutes were in line and running concentrically.

Another 'Archifact' on the same theme is in Cocobolo, shown in Photo 19, being 63mm 2½" ø x 425mm 16¾" tall. After form-turning and polishing, the through-cavity was roughed out with ball-end mills and finished off with the special cutter previously mentioned going in vertically from both sides in turn. The outer 'fluting' was produced by the same tool, but with the product revolved 180° on the dividing plate. In machining these side cuts, the compound curves near the base were formed naturally when the cutting ceased.

The most elaborate and time-consuming piece I have made so far is shown in Photos 20 and 20A — in She Oak which, my conscience is frequently telling me, was originally a billet 125mm 5" sqr. x 460mm 18" long! It now has a base of 50mm 2" ø x 120mm 4¾" at its widest x 450mm 17¾" tall and about 3mm ⅛" at its thinnest near the top. It is not a very happy wood to work with, being prone to splintering and tearing. The basic form was turned and much of the 'flat-on-the-twist' was hacked away on the mill, followed by much more hacking, smoothing and finishing by hand. The reward, however, is a good finish and quite dramatic grain figuring. Although the cut-out feature in the surface had been planned, it did also eliminate two nasty tears which would otherwise have marred the product!

'I have always wanted to make a piece which shows what the inside of the wood looks like.'

There are four 'Archifacts' which do not feature any helical form at all — see Photos 21, 22, 23 and 24 . . . and in numerical order, the one on the left is the only one which has received no machining at all — just a long, long exercise by hand. It is 420mm 16½" tall in

Photo 21

Purple Heart. Number 2 is also in P.H., is 430mm 17" tall and is a simple turned project with the 'cap' eccentrically integral. Next along is 'Smiler' on 95mm 3¾" ø base with a 90mm 3½" ø sphere and standing 485mm 19" tall, in Bubinga with its very

Photo 22

distinctive graining, and finally a piece of Kingwood, 70mm 2¾" ø x 290mm 11½" as a simple exercise in eccentric turning.

Leather

As a final gesture, it seems fitting that the natural virtues of wood should be complemented by an equally natural material to stand on and 'Archifacts' are lined with leather. It needs to be quite thin to provide a firm base

Photo 23

and skives from good quality skins work well — real kid would be even better. Most leathers will rag slightly and show their natural colour at the edges after trimming, but a spirit pen to match the wood does the trick.

First the 12mm ½" hole is plugged and pared flush and a slight indent made in its centre to take the centre point of a 32mm 1¼" ø wad cutter. With the product held against the cutter spinning in the lathe, a neat disc will be cut and of course, the same cutter can be used to produce a protected label bearing details of the wood, date, etc. Contact adhesive is used in both cases.

I will not quote the too well-worn cliché about limitations and imagination. Suffice to say that the few pieces I have made represent a mere surface scratch on the potential for producing 'Archifacts' and the like, by the machining methods described and illustrated.■

Photo 24

LESS IS MORE

Daniel Ellegiers suggests how woodturners can play around with ideas in order to produce more than simply balusters, bowls and boxes.

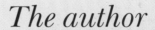

In the evolution of architecture and furniture, Mies van der Rohe (1886-1969) occupies a special place. He reduced form and space to simple and pure lines and launched the principle that less is more.

Woodturners do not need to have the pretention to do the same thing in their field of applied art. But, with Mies van der Rohe's vision in mind, turners can take advantage of his views and way of thinking to do some interesting experiments.

The pleasure of woodturning lies not only in making, but also in designing. It is not easy to come up with new designs. For originality a woodturner has to try to free the mind of traditional woodturning themes.

Extras

The main thing is to get rid of the idea that a lathe can only turn balusters, legs, bowls, platters or boxes. To these traditional items can be added external or internal artistic extras such as carving, painting or marquetry.

You can also start from the round form and find out what can be done with this, the basic form of turning. You can transform the round shape into geometrical figures using a jigsaw, for example.

Start by sawing in a shallow platter just a plain line the length of the

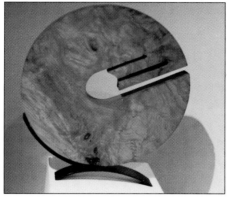

Less is More, an Ellegiers-inspired idea from Shirley Thomas.

> **'The pleasure of woodturning lies not only in making, but also in designing'.**

radius, ending in a small circular shape. From there, play with that line, for example is that line a mouth? Add other lines a nose, a chin, an eye, or whatever you think it to be. It can be the start of a creative and pleasant play of the mind. It is drawing forms in space – drawing forms in the air.

However, keep also in mind the answer Paul Venturi gave to the views of Mies van der Rohe: less is a bore!

Two simple ideas from Daniel Ellegiers.

The author

Dr Daniel Ellegiers, 74, was born in Westrozebeke, Belgium, and is a man of wide education and experience. He received several bursaries for scientific research during his early career, and was a lecturer at the University of Osaka, Japan, in the early 1950s before returning to take professorships at universities in Belgium.

He was Deputy Commissioner-General of the Belgian Government from 1969-71.

In retirement Prof Ellegiers enjoys teaching and demonstrating woodturning, as well as producing his own work at his home in Gevere-Vurste, Belgium.

Shirley Thomas from New Zealand has been in correspondence with Daniel Ellegiers and shared his ideas with a woodturning friend, Irwin.

She writes: "We put a piece of wood on the lathe, turned it true and made a hole in the centre. Then, with much discussion of proportion and alignment, we made a cut across the grain. The result is the photo enclosed.

"Irwin and his friend David also had creative fun with Prof. Ellegiers ideas, and each made a wonderful piece. Irwin entered his in an exhibition recently and it drew much comment, though the judges nearly disqualified it.

"Vic Wood saw it and wrote to Irwin about how he really liked it. Irwin's friend David took his piece to Otematata for a critique. It was amazing how many were drawn to it".

Sliding stock

John Warner tells you how to save money on a lever-operated tailstock by making your own

Having a batch of pepper mills to make which needed a 25mm, 1in hole drilled through, I regretted not having bought the optional lever-operated tailstock when I purchased my Jubilee lathe, in 1950.

The cost then was just out of my reach, and is still beyond my purse now that they are available again.

The large hand-wheel on the standard tailstock is quite efficient, but takes time to wind back, and there is only 75mm, 3in of travel.

I suddenly thought that it might be possible to slide the whole tailstock instead of just the quill.

I made a few sketches and decided what was required. The lever had to go in the direction I wanted the tailstock to go, with as much travel as possible. And it had to be made of wood and easy to build, with few parts.

I made a mock-up from strips of softwood and panel pins, altering the lengths until I found the best combination. I have not given dimensions here, as they are better worked out to suit your lathe and needs.

First problem

The first problem was how to connect the tailstock to the lever. A pivot had to be on the centreline of the lathe to give an even thrust. A bolted-on block of oak was the answer.

Cast-iron is surprisingly easy to drill, almost like wood. I used medium density fibreboard (MDF) to make the fixing plate or base, bolted to the bed with a length of 13mm, ½in diameter threaded rod.

A captive nut underneath enabled me to fix the assembly anywhere along the lathe bed. Plywood, hardwood, or even metal, could also be used.

The levers are made from European beech (*Fagus sylvatica*) and pivoted

A mock-up allows details to be worked out, such as the lengths of the levers and the pivot positions to give the right travel.

The underside of the fixing plate or base. A captive nut on the end of a length of threaded rod clamps the base in place.

LEFT: **A wedge holds the tail-stock lever in place. The wood extending past the tailstock is marked, so a pin on the pivot block shows the depth of the drill.**

Silicone spray lubricant helps the tailstock slide smoothly.

The underside of the tailstock, showing the oak pivot block bolted in place.

with metal kitchen cabinet connectors, the type where a bolt fits a sleeve nut. Regular nuts and bolts could also be used, with washers for spacers.

The pivot to the tailstock block is loose, so it can be removed quickly. It's impossible to get a screwdriver to it, anyway.

All that remained was to see if it worked. It did first time, with no need for alterations.

The method of use is to set up the drill with the drill in the headstock, rest the wood to be drilled against the tip of the drill, then bring up the tailstock to the starting position. Without moving the tailstock, the lever mechanism is place in position and its base clamped to the lathe bed.

I wedge the tailstock-clamping-lever in position and bring up the toolrest to stop the wood revolving with the drill. Make sure the drill and tailstock points are in the correct position, set the speed, start the lathe and pull the lever.

The gadget's main advantage over the hand wheel is that although the feed speed is the same, you can only go as fast as the drill will cut. The bigger the drill diameter, the slower the rpm – remember, 'steady feed, slow speed.' ➤

Set up and ready to drill a block for a flute. The toolrest stops the block rotating.

I've used my lever many times now, and have found it well worth the effort. This is the marvellous thing about woodturning – no matter how many years you have been at it, you can always find new ways and methods to improve the quality or finish of the work and, hopefully, speed things up as well. ■

Drilling a block for a pepper mill. Note the pivoting end of the lever supported on packing blocks to clear the clamping bolt.

The author

John Warner is a woodturner and carver who lives at St.Germans, Saltash, Cornwall.
If any manufacturer would like to market his lever-operated tailstock, they can contact him on 01503 230129.

➤ To withdraw the wood to clear the waste and return to cutting is almost instantaneous. The lever also allows you to drill much deeper without resetting, up to 200mm, 8in without repositioning the base, or 400mm, 16in if the blank is drilled from both ends.

Smoother slide

Another problem to overcome was locking the tailstock lever so the tailstock could slide smoothly without lifting – a squirt of silicon spray on the lathe bed helped.

Although slightly crude, a wedge-shaped hardwood block drilled through to fit over the handle worked quite well.

The last task was to add a depth-measuring gauge. This is simply a strip of wood screwed to the baseplate and marked in millimetres or inches, with a nail in the oak block as a pointer.

I always drill the hole before turning pepper mills, holding the drill in a Jacob's chuck in the headstock, with the wood square or octagonal. The toolrest stops the wood from turning.

RIGHT: **The components of the tailstock lever, minus the pivot block, which remains on the tailstock.**

My poleless pole lathe was a pleasure to make. Cheap and easy to build, it is light, yet stable, folds neatly away, and is a fun way to keep fit.

Basically, it's a pole lathe where the overhead pole has been replaced by a bungee cord. This is hooked under the left foot and attached to a cord which passes over a pulley.

The cord is then wrapped around the workpiece twice and fixed through a hole near the end of a foot-operated piece of broomstick. The stick is hinged on a strong screw through the other end.

Mastering the skew on this lathe is character building, the secret of success being to withdraw the chisel slightly whenever you raise your leg.

The main parts you will need are given in the panel. The centres, placed

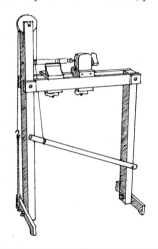

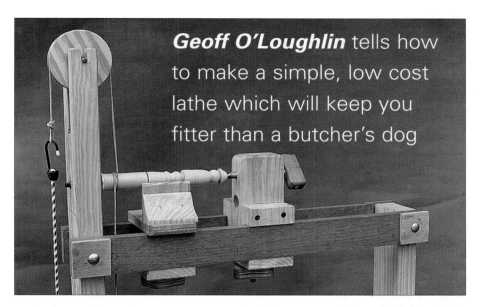

Geoff O'Loughlin tells how to make a simple, low cost lathe which will keep you fitter than a butcher's dog

The top half of the lathe.

Poleless pole lathe

90mm, 3½in above the bed, are made from 13mm, ½in thread rod.

An easy way to point one end is to put the rod in an electric drill and hold it while rotating. Do this first against a bench grindstone to shape the point, then against fine wet and dry sandpaper to get a polished finish.

The tailstock and toolrest – both made from pine – are clamped to the bed using a washer and a nut embedded in car body filler in a plywood handle which has been shaped on the bandsaw.

The tailstock centre, which is a tight friction fit, has a wooden adjusting handle. This was fitted by drilling a 6mm, ¼in hole through the length of the handle and through the end of the threaded rod. It is fixed in a piece of 6mm, ¼in rod using body filler.

The hole seen below the tailstock centre is to give access for a nut to be fixed with body filler to the threaded rod used for clamping the tailstock down.

The toolrest is a piece of plywood glued to a support. The top is 6mm, ¼in below the centre height. The tailstock and toolrest dimensions are not critical, but the former should be a good sliding fit. ■

Main parts

Left leg (pine)	1,270 x 90 x 45mm, 50 x 3½ x 1¾in
Right leg (pine)	940 x 90 x 45mm, 37 x 3½ x 1¾in
Bed, 2 pieces (hardwood)	710 x 63 x 19mm, 28 x 2½ x ¾in
Feet, 2 pieces (hardwood)	380 x 63 x 19mm, 15 x 2½ x ¾in
4 squares (plywood)	63 x 63 x 6mm, 2½ x 2½ x ¼in
The squares are glued to the bed ends to prevent possible splitting when the nuts are tightened	
2 coach bolts (for bed)	150 x 5mm, 6 x ³⁄₁₆in
2 coach bolts (for feet)	75 x 5mm, 3 x ³⁄₁₆in
1 coach bolt (for toolrest)	127 x 12mm, 5 x ½in
Dowel	32mm dia x 750mm, 1¼ x 29½in
Pulley wheel (plywood)	19 x 108mm dia, ¾ x 4¼in
Axle (steel rod)	6 x 75mm L, ¼ x 3in
This rod is a press fit in the wheel and rests in the leg as shown	

BITS 'N' PIECES

HUGH McKAY

Hugh McKay's original ideas for embellishing his turned vessels led him to design a more flexible ornamental lathe system, which he describes here.

D on't get me wrong. I admire a lot of the symmetrical work I've seen created with an ornamental lathe. But my 'wilder' designs — suggested by nature — for decorating turned forms called for a simpler, more flexible system.

After hours of running ideas through my head and building several prototypes, I came up with a system which works fairly well for shaping the outside of a piece and also makes it easy to control the wall thickness of a vase. The sides can be carved away without worrying about removing too much wood and going through the side.

I use a router-type tool and bit held rigidly, but which can still be moved back and forth from the turning's surface.

The bit is pushed into the wood to be removed and pulled back to allow that which is to remain to pass.

I use a large pneumatic die grinder for the power source, mainly because it is much slimmer than any electric counterpart of equivalent power. I built a jig to hold the die grinder parallel to the surface it sits on.

The apparatus fits into the other part of the system. This part holds the die grinder jig snug, but still allows it to slide easily back and forth (Photo 1).

I am not going to explain here how to make this die grinder jig/sliding system. The photos should give anyone

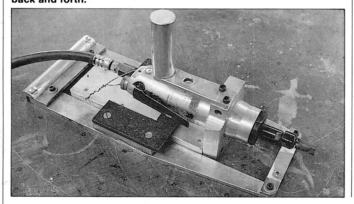

Photo 1 The die grinder jig is held snug, but can still slide back and forth.

with average skills enough information to build their own.

It is made from aluminium and a type of Teflon plastic for ease of sliding. I am sure someone else could come up with a better system, but mine does work.

To operate it, a platform is needed to run the die grinder on. This platform needs a small amount of vertical movement to align things properly with different operations.

I use a built-in platform holder with the lathe's toolrest holder. The post which fits into the toolrest has a steel ring of slightly larger diameter welded to it.

A large rectangular steel plate is bolted to that ring. By shimming between the rectangular plate and the welded ring, the platform can be adjusted level to the turning.

Even though the system is simpler, it still has to be accurate (Photo 2).

The final steel plate has two

Photo 2 Even though the system is simpler, it still has to be accurate.

holes drilled and tapped at opposite ends to allow a piece of plywood to be bolted to it. This is the platform surface the die grinder jig slides on.

The plywood needs to fit close to the turning, the approximate shape of the turned form being cut out of it (Photo 3). This shows work on a piece called *Star*.

This platform must be the appropriate width to allow the

Photo 3 The approximate shape of the turned form *Star* is cut out of the plywood.

die grinder jig to fit on it and also move the jig around the turning.

The plywood is used to clamp the jig to it and holds it solid while the tool bit is plunged into the wood (Photo 4).

To control the depth of cut, I use 3mm 1/8" masonite as a template to hold the jig against. The masonite is cut to roughly

Photo 4 The tool bit is plunged into the wood.

fit against the outside of the turning, attached to the plywood platform with two or three screws.

Then I carefully go around the turning, marking equidistant points from the outside of the form to the determined width that the template needs to be.

You end up with the template shape the same as the turning's but usually 50-100mm 2-4″ larger than the turning's diameter.

This template is painted gloss black and is between the turning and the die grinder.

The initial removal of wood now begins and you can see some of the areas of design taking shape (Photos 5 and 6).

Photo 5 The initial removal of wood begins.

Photo 6 The design begins to take shape.

The type of router bit used in the die grinder depends on what needs to be done. I might use a ¾″ flat bit if a smooth surface is wanted or lots of wood is to be removed.

Depending on the detail of the design, ⅛″, ³⁄₁₆″, or ¼″ bits can be used. If I want the design to flow from the turning's surface a round nose bit is used. If I want the design to
▶

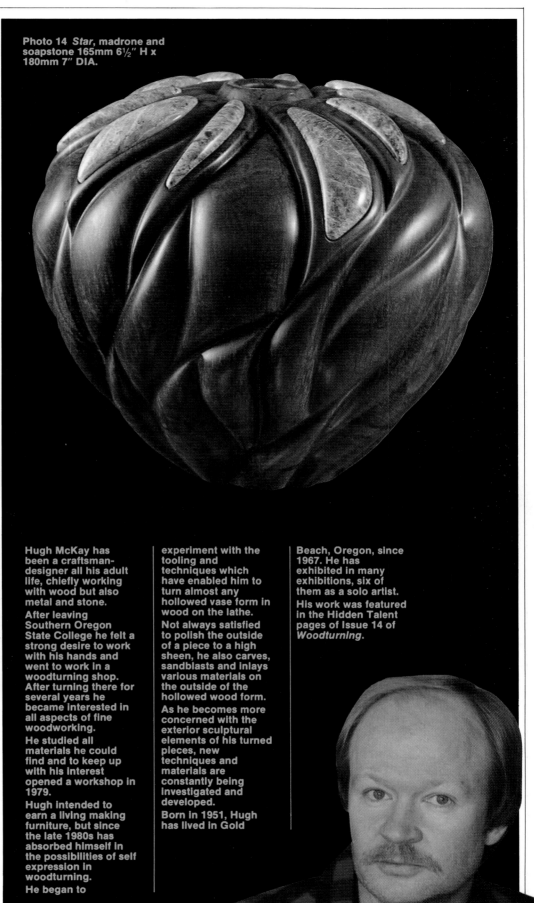

Photo 14 *Star*, madrone and soapstone 165mm 6½″ H x 180mm 7″ DIA.

Hugh McKay has been a craftsman-designer all his adult life, chiefly working with wood but also metal and stone.

After leaving Southern Oregon State College he felt a strong desire to work with his hands and went to work in a woodturning shop. After turning there for several years he became interested in all aspects of fine woodworking.

He studied all materials he could find and to keep up with his interest opened a workshop in 1979.

Hugh intended to earn a living making furniture, but since the late 1980s has absorbed himself in the possibilities of self expression in woodturning.

He began to experiment with the tooling and techniques which have enabled him to turn almost any hollowed vase form in wood on the lathe.

Not always satisfied to polish the outside of a piece to a high sheen, he also carves, sandblasts and inlays various materials on the outside of the hollowed wood form.

As he becomes more concerned with the exterior sculptural elements of his turned pieces, new techniques and materials are constantly being investigated and developed.

Born in 1951, Hugh has lived in Gold Beach, Oregon, since 1967. He has exhibited in many exhibitions, six of them as a solo artist.

His work was featured in the Hidden Talent pages of Issue 14 of *Woodturning*.

seem slightly separate from the turned form, a flat bottom bit leaves a decisive corner.

After shaping the outside of the turned form with gouge and/or scrapers, the hollowing out process begins.

I carefully remove the insides of the turning until the correct wall thickness is reached. This is determined by the depth the finished design is to be plus the finished wall thickness.

For example, if the outside carving is to be 12mm ½″ deep and the finished wall thickness 6mm ¼″, the vase would be hollowed out with a 20mm ¾″ wall thickness. The vessel is now ready to have its surface design carved.

I usually rough out a design on paper before drawing the final design on the turning with a soft lead pencil. A lot of my design time is spent erasing lines until things look right.

The final design must take into consideration the wood itself — its grain, soft spots, holes and other 'flaws'. Once the drawing is completed, the piece is remounted on the lathe and the die grinder system set up.

This carving technique or 'slow-speed lathe turning' allows a type of carving that would be hard to do without using the die grinder system with the lathe. A very deep and, if called for, intricate type of carving can be done, a bit like laser carvings.

After this 'roughing out' work

with the die grinder the turning is parted off the faceplate and clean-up work begins.

Completion of the carved design is done with a small die grinder and rotary mills. Carving tools, rasps, files and sandpaper are also used if needed (Photo 7).

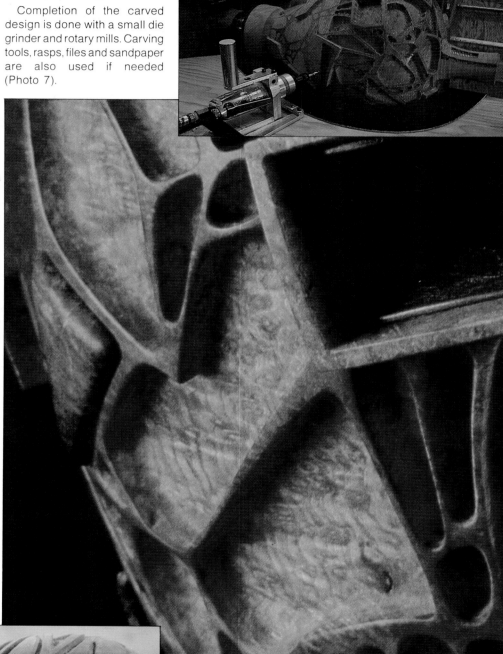

Photo 7 Carving tools are also used if necessary.

I often sandblast a piece such as *Aeon* (Photos 8-13). In preparation for this, the high areas are coated with silicone caulk to protect them from the sand.

The light coloured compound you see is where soapstone will be inlaid (Photo 11).

This compound is used to protect the area from sand-blasting, and also as models to help me shape and fit the soapstone to the wood later.

After sandblasting, the final polishing and fitting of the sandcast lead and soapstone elements are completed. All design elements are then glued

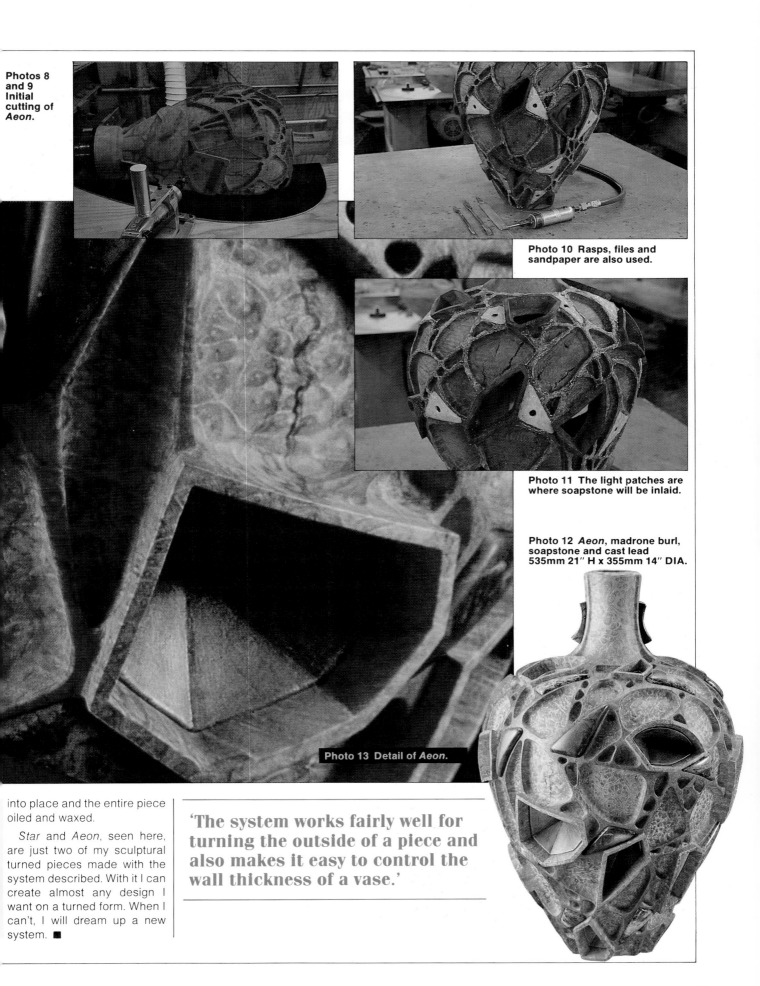

Photos 8 and 9 Initial cutting of *Aeon*.

Photo 10 Rasps, files and sandpaper are also used.

Photo 11 The light patches are where soapstone will be inlaid.

Photo 12 *Aeon*, madrone burl, soapstone and cast lead 535mm 21″ H x 355mm 14″ DIA.

Photo 13 Detail of *Aeon*.

into place and the entire piece oiled and waxed.

Star and *Aeon*, seen here, are just two of my sculptural turned pieces made with the system described. With it I can create almost any design I want on a turned form. When I can't, I will dream up a new system. ∎

'The system works fairly well for turning the outside of a piece and also makes it easy to control the wall thickness of a vase.'

BEST BOBBIN BLUEPRINT

David Springett explains what makes a good working lace bobbin.

Judges in our lace bobbin turning competition (*Woodturning*, Issue 35) made the comment that though the bobbins were all nicely turned, many would not work well, as the head shape was wrong.

This resulted in several readers asking, "What **is** the right shape"? So, in this article, I'll tell you what makes a good working bobbin.

A lace bobbin is a tool and must function perfectly to be acceptable. When it does, the rest of the shaping and decoration can be as wild and exciting as the turner's imagination.

The body of the bobbin is the handle. This is where it is picked up, keeping any dirt or grease from the fingers off the thread.

The thread is wrapped round the bobbin neck, which must have sufficient length and diameter to take plenty of thread. Some lace patterns require a lot of thread.

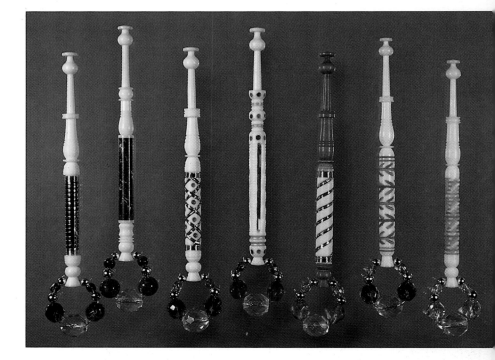

Bone bobbins (left to right), Bobby Dazzler, Crushed Velvet, Double Fairing, Grandmother (a slim 6mm, ¼" bobbin inside which there's a smaller bobbin with another minute one inside that), Dyed Fairing, Arrows, and Tutti Frutti.

The head

East Midland style bobbins (the most popular type) have a second neck on the head. The thread is stored wound round the main neck then comes up on to the head to be fixed round the short neck with a double hitch. This is to prevent the thread unwinding unexpectedly and allows controlled uncoiling.

The Devon style bobbin has a single pancake head, and the double hitch is made just below the head.

There are many head shapes for bobbins, each bobbin maker developing his or her own. The look of the bobbin head is not as important as that it works well.

Bear in mind the lace bobbin's function. The thread is wound on the neck and unwound as required. The double hitch lets the bobbin hang on the lace maker's pillow. It's important that the head design allows this.

Heads that won't hold the thread, causing the bobbin to slip from the pillow and unravel the thread, are all but useless.

On all styles of bobbin it's important that the edge of the head is smooth, as this is where the thread leaves the bobbin for good. A sharp edge can weaken and cut thread.

The spangle is the ring of beads on the tail of the East Midlands lace bobbin. It adds weight and prevents the bobbin from rolling about on the pillow and tangling threads.

Delicate work

Turning a lace bobbin is delicate work and calls for a light touch. It takes time to understand how much weight to give to the tool. Don't be dismayed if you break your first few attempts. Persevere, it does get easier.

It's important that the head is perfectly smooth, as any dents, dimples or cracks will catch the thread, making the bobbin difficult and annoying to use.

Try to get a clean finish from the tools. I do use abrasive paper on a fin-

Bobbins by David Springett, lace by his wife, Christine.

A variety of wooden bobbins, including Leopards, Tigers, Butterflies, Bees Knees, Curved Bitted, and others.

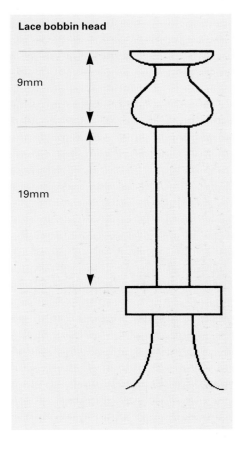

Lace bobbin head

9mm

19mm

...shed head, but only a light touch to remove whiskers. Too much sanding removes the delicacy of the turning.

If you overdo it with the sand paper the finished work will look as though it has been squeezed rather than turned. Crispness of turning is what raises a bobbin from fair to superb.

Try to develop a head shape you like, but make sure it works well. You should be able to find plenty of eager lacemakers to test your bobbins, and they will quickly let you know how good or bad they are.

● For more details on lace bobbin turning David Springett has written a book on the subject. *Turning Lace Bobbins* is published by C & D Springett, 21 Hillmorton Road, Rugby, Warwicks CV22 5DF. It costs

The lace bobbin

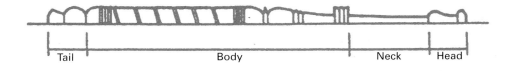

Tail   Body   Neck   Head

£12.75 (plus £2.25 p&p, £5.50 overseas).

● The bobbins made for our bobbin turning competition last year are being put to good use. Alan Hewitt, bobbin maker demonstrator at The Old Stores Turnery, in Nantwich, Cheshire, and one of the judges, will be auctioning them at his demonstrations. The proceeds from the sale will be given to charity.

Our thanks to Alan Holtham and staff for preparing the mopane blanks for the competition and providing such an interesting challenge.

If you would like to get more mopane (which proved easy to turn and carve) or other exotic timbers contact: The Old Stores Turnery, Wistaston Road, Willaston, Nantwich, Cheshire. Tel: 01270 67010. ■

Top view of the completed bowl, showing the large split that opened up during torching.

PUT TO THE TORCH

Roger Parry tells how he 'aged' a bowl with a blow-torch, creating a charred effect

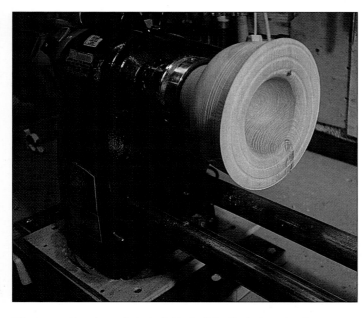

The turned bowl, ready to be 'attacked' by the butane torch

My friends were not to be caught out when I showed them a wooden bowl and asked each of them how old it was? They all agreed it looked hundreds of years old, but added that as I'd asked the question, I must have recently made it."

They were right! The bowl was not even 24 hours old. What I'd done was to age my bowl by setting fire to it.

Challenging

An enthusiastic amateur woodturner, I sometimes like to try something more challenging and different from my usual work.

Having toyed with the idea of making something with an experimental finish, I decided it should be a 'medieval' bowl, finished to look as though it was made in 1396.

I selected an ash log that had spent two or three years weathering in the garden and had dried inside the workshop for a further year. The wood's texture felt dry and feathery, which made me feel it was on the verge of rotting.

Intuition told me it should turn easily, be flame-torched effectively and 'feel' right. After all, a 'medieval' bowl that felt too heavy and hard, with crisp decorative work, would not look right.

Preparation

The bowl blank, measuring 190 x 100mm, 7 ½ x 4in, was prepared on the band saw and mounted on the lathe, using a combination chuck with the screw chuck attachment.

As I'd hoped, the bowl turned easily. I used a 10mm, ⅜in spindle gouge to shape the outside, until it looked right. The side wall slightly flared to the lip to create a fairly sharp edge I later intended to burn off.

Just under the lip I placed four or five decorative grooves, 3mm, ⅛in apart, using the long point of a 25mm, 1in skew chisel.

I tapered the base to about 75mm, 3in diameter and prepared the foot with a 50 x 3mm, 2 x ⅛in spigot, in readiness for the next operation. There was no need to sand the surface, because the surface was later to be burnt off.

The workpiece was reversed and held using the 50mm, 2 in spigot collet in the combination chuck and a recess turned in the top. I chose a recess shape like that inside a pestle and left

▶

The start of the charring process.

The process nearly complete. Don't hold the torch too close to the work, as the flame and the heat can blow back and extinguish the flame.

the walls quite thick. There was no academic reason for this, it simply looked right.

I shallowly rounded the top edge and tapered it into the recess. Finally, I decorated with a spiral, starting at the edge and disappearing into the gloomy depths of the inner hole.

This was amateurishly done, with a 6mm, ¼ in spindle gouge, turning the bowl slowly by hand and following a pencilled guide line, drawn and modified until it looked like a fairly even spiral.

Shallow

I did this operation several times, taking shallow cuts to avoid dig-ins and ensuring the groove was neither too deep nor wide.

When I was satisfied, I sanded the groove sparingly with 240 grit abrasive paper. This was bent over to form a radiused 'fold,' to fit the groove. I turned the bowl by hand until tool marks and sharp edges had disappeared.

I now vacuum-cleaned the lathe, workbench and workshop floor, removing wood shavings and dust, to reduce fire risk during my favourite part of the operation.

With the bowl still in place on the spigot collet and the lathe switched off, I lit a butane torch and adjusted the flame so no yellow flame and not too much bright blue flame could be seen.

It's essential not to have too fierce a flame, or the wood closest to the torch would burn away while the surrounding wood would not even be charred.

Using my left hand to slowly rotate the bowl by handling the chuck and not the bowl itself, I aimed the flame at the edge and front of the bowl.

I continued this until the bowl was quite evenly, but not too heavily, charred. The fact that the edges caught fire and red glowing embers could be seen did not make me panic, as I needed the edges to be

fairly heavily charred in places.

When I felt enough burning had taken place, I removed the flame from the wood and turned off the butane torch for safety reasons.

On the subject of safety, I strongly advise you to keep a bucket of water and a mug or tin can handy, in case the flames get out of hand.

Dirty stage

The next stage was very dirty, and overalls, dust mask, cap and eye protection were essential. I used a piece of worn out terry-towelling about 460mm, 18 in square which proved to be ideal for this operation.

I switched on the lathe at 450 rpm and, with the towelling, rubbed off the excess charcoal. I repeated the flaming and cleaning until I was happy with the depth of colour.

By concentrating the flame on certain areas, I

found the shape of edges and grooves could be controlled quite well.

During this operation, the bowl emitted violent cracking, hissing and splitting noises, as the wood reacted to the extreme concentrations of heat.

When splits and cracks appeared, I made sure all fresh 'white' wood soon disappeared under the flame.

Eventually, I was satisfied with the overall effect. The new surface looked quite different from the original bowl, with the edges nicely rounded off and blunted.

The decorative grooves had the distorted look of railway lines in a desert, while the spiral ones now had that battered look associated with years of use and abuse. A lovely crack had appeared, cutting right across one side of the top edge.

This crack had opened quite wide when the heat was applied, so the edges

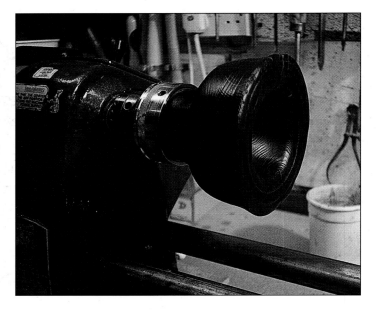

Side view of bowl.

were nicely burnt away and the inside had turned a deep brown. During the cooling process it closed a little, and ended looking like an ancient working injury.

The stage at which I began to suspect the bowl had nearly finished 'cooking' was when the colour could no longer be made darker without masses of yellow flame converting the wood to barbecue fuel.

Burnt

I wanted the wood to be burnt dark brown, but to remain solid enough to take a polish.

The bowl was now beginning to look a young 'medieval.' It only needed a 'patina' to complete the illusion of age.

I'd observed that a patina not only had a natural polished look or lustre, but that the lustre had depth. I needed a method that would create this depth as well as the lustre.

Having already made my own wax polish from woodturning books which extolled the virtues of beeswax, carnauba wax and pure turpentine, I applied this to the warm wood and let it melt into the grain.

By applying a little wax,

The polished bowl. Only the foot remains to be turned, scorched and polished. Note the water container – just in case.

polishing it off and occasionally re-warming the wood, letting the wax melt deep into it, I eventually achieved a finish I felt would pass for an antique lustre.

All that remained to do, was to re-chuck the bowl using a modified four-jaw chuck with homemade adjustable jaws. Holding the bowl by the rim, I turned off the spigot,

slightly dishing the foot.

I then flamed and patina'd the finished foot to blend with the rest of the bowl and finally burnished the whole with a clean piece of terry- towelling.

The 'medieval' bowl now has pride of place in my living room and is a frequent talking point with visiting friends. I always ask them: "How old do you think this bowl is?" ∎

The author

Roger Parry was born in Middlesex in 1945 and was introduced to woodturning at school.

His next encounter with it was 28 years later, using a Black & Decker lathe attachment with a home-made headstock and a ⅛hp washing machine motor. But his turning was curtailed by the pressure of work demanded by a newsagents and general store he bought in Cornwall.

Four years ago, following a move to Rutland, he bought a cheap Taiwanese lathe and determined to learn woodturning properly. Many hours and much determination later – not to mention demonstrations, lectures, the Warwick seminar, books and videos and a regular subscription to *Woodturning* magazine – he is starting to delve into surface texturing and finishing.

MAKING A CHEAP LATHE BETTER

ANDY BARNES

Like many other beginners, when Andy Barnes started woodturning he bought a cheap Taiwanese lathe. This was adequate, but its limitations soon became apparent, so he made a number of modifications which he describes here.

Andy Barnes was introduced to woodworking at preparatory school, but only became 'hooked' on woodturning after attending a Craft Supplies open day two years ago.

Attempting to make an egg cup under the expert tuition of Keith Rowley, he had almost completed it when he decided to make one more 'finishing' cut, against Keith's better judgment.

He caught an edge and the cup disintegrated. But his enthusiasm was unshaken. He bought Keith's book, *Woodturning, A Foundation Course*, a 10mm ⅜" spindle gouge and a bag of wood and dashed home to set up an electric drill lathe and try his hand, turning another egg cup, successfully this time.

Andy, 32, studied mechanical engineering before doing a variety of jobs. He is now a senior systems analyst with Barclays Bank. He is married with two children.

A nature lover, he derives great satisfaction from turning a discarded log into a thing of beauty.

It was turning an egg cup at one of Craft Supplies open days that did it. From then I was hooked on woodturning. I soon realised that I needed a proper lathe with different speeds, a moveable tailstock and a reliable toolrest.

I decided on a NU Tool lathe, from Taiwan, mainly because of the price, and found it adequate, though by no means perfect. I have since made a number of modifications to suit my own needs. These are:

● The addition of an electric cut-out switch on the drive cover door.

● A short lever added to the cover door catch.

● A shortened bed, enabling the tailstock to be swung out of the way.

● Fitting the tailstock with an external wheel.

Taking each in order, I shall describe them in more detail.

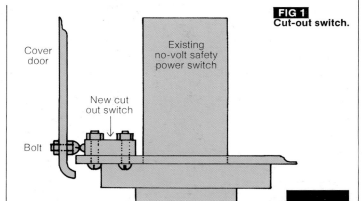

FIG 1
Cut-out switch.

Cover door

New cut out switch

Existing no-volt safety power switch

Bolt

The cut-out switch and door catch.

Cut-out switch

The cut-out switch came from an electric shower pressure sensor — but they are readily available. I mounted the switch beside the lathe's on/off switch (FIG 1).

It was connected to the live wire between the no-volt safety switch and the mains. The switch was closed by a small bolt in the drive cover door.

Drive cover catch

To make the drive cover easier to open, which I don't recommend without first fitting a cut-out switch, I brazed 50mm 2" of 3mm ⅛" bar to the nut that keeps the door shut. Simple as that.

Shortened bed

As the NU Tool lathe comes with its bed in two halves I decided to use only one half so it would fit better on my workbench. This was a temporary arrangement, since the bracket to hold the end of ▶

the bar bed was not properly located.

I then used a 100mm 4" section cut from the second bar bed and fitted it between the first bed bar and the bracket. Everything became much more solid.

This arrangement has another great advantage — it allows the tailstock to be rotated out of the way, as the short length of bed bar does not have the key running underneath it (FIG 2).

All that is needed to make this conversion is a 125mm 5" bolt and a metalwork saw. Once it is done the lathe has an effective between centres length of 405mm 16". Using the longer bed bar the between centres length is 840mm 33".

One point to note. The inside of the second bed bar is machined parallel on its internal diameter. You can cut off the 100mm 4" section from either end.

If you use the machined end you can fit it straight on the lathe, but if you want to use the longer bed bar it would be difficult to machine.

I cut the 100mm 4" from the non-machined end and had it trued up and the internal diameter machined parallel by a professional.

Outside wheel for the tailstock

One of the few things I found

of warning — you should not attempt this work if the inside of the tailstock casting looks in any way suspect.

To true up the outside faces I used a file to remove the bulk of the waste and to finish made use of a small, round piece of plywood with 60 grit sandpaper glued to it.

The wood was attached to a length of 12mm ½" DIA steel bar held in a Jacob's chuck. The lathe was started at its slowest speed and the tailstock

FIG 2 New tailstock arrangement.

Tailstock position for turning between centres

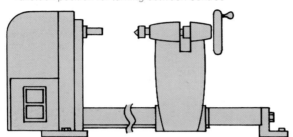

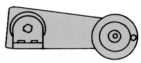

Tailstock position for bowl turning

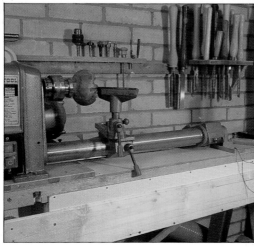

Lathe in spindle turning mode, i.e. with tailstock support. Note dust extraction pipe and tool holder.

Lathe in bowl turning mode (with tailstock rotated out of the way).

Truing up the faces of the tailstock.

really annoying about my lathe was the tailstock wheel, which I couldn't advance quickly or fluidly.

To put the wheel on the outside so you can achieve this movement you need two pieces machining and the tailstock casting needs truing up.

The internal bore on my tailstock was well cast, so I had no need to change it, but the faces were very rough. A word

gently moved against the block.

Cutting is slow and the dirty cast iron dust needs to be removed from the sandpaper regularly. By reversing the wood and pulling the tailstock you can face the edge furthest from the headstock (FIG 3).

Only the two edges furthest away need to be trued, but I trued up all four faces — it doesn't take long.

One problem occurred when

FIG 3 Preparing for tailstock wheel.

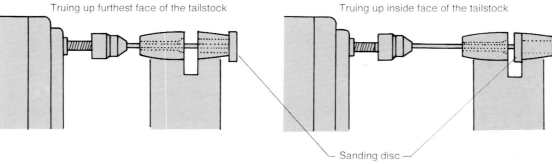

Truing up furthest face of the tailstock   Truing up inside face of the tailstock

— Sanding disc —

Truing up the faces of the tailstock, using the rest to keep the chuck in position.

The new bits for the tailstock, including grub screw on retaining collar, pock marked surface of sleeve (a first attempt to stop wheel slipping), and retaining screw for handle (best method to stop wheel slipping).

the tailstock was pulled away from the headstock — it tended to pull the chuck out since it was a morse taper fit.

I got round the problem by using the toolrest to bear against the chuck body with some grease to lubricate it all.

'One of the few things I found really annoying about my lathe was the tailstock wheel, which I couldn't advance quickly or fluidly.'

The October 1993 issue of **Woodturning** contained a tip which described a safer method of holding a Jacob's chuck, but you may be lucky enough to have a chuck that fits directly to the headstock spindle, a much better arrangement.

The two parts needed are shown in FIG 4 — a threaded

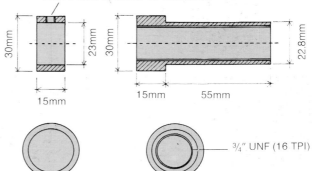

2 BA thread or similar for lock screw

30mm   23mm   30mm   22.8mm

15mm   15mm   55mm

¾" UNF (16 TPI)

FIG 4 Threaded and locking sleeve for the tailstock.

sleeve and a locking sleeve. I would check the internal diameter bore of the tailstock and adjust accordingly. Mine has a 29mm inside diameter.

Also note that the internal thread must be machined parallel to the outside of the sleeve — otherwise it will not work well, if at all.

Then get the parts machined, or even better do it yourself if you can. I found someone who would do it in their lunch hour for a nominal fee.

The next part was to make the wheel. I used a piece of 32mm 1¼" thick pine board, mounted it on a faceplate and bored a hole in the middle to make a good fit with the sleeve.

After one side of the wheel was shaped it was removed from the faceplate and fitted to the sleeve, which was screwed on to the headstock spindle so the other side could be turned.

Once the wheel was finished a hole was drilled in the edge to take a small handle which had been drilled and turned. It was attached with a long bolt, secured with a nut (FIG 5).

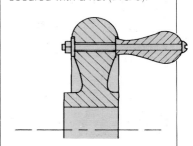

FIG 5 Handle bolted to new tailstock wheel.

To assemble was fairly easy. I first removed the tailstock spindle, then inserted the new sleeve with the wheel attached from the far end, fitted the locking sleeve in the middle and adjusted it so the wheel ▶

turned easily without catching.

I adjusted the lock screw so it was just holding, inserted the tailstock spindle from the headstock end and screwed it through. If the end waggles as you screw it up, you have a problem, as the internal thread is not parallel with the outside of the sleeve. Time for a new sleeve.

Assuming everything is OK, the next job is to tighten the lock screw, though not too tight or the threaded sleeve will distort and you won't be able to move the spindle.

I have learnt many things from having a lathe, but one thing I would especially like to pass on — if you bolt your lathe to a workbench bolted to a wall there may be less vibration, but it causes two other big problems.

First, sound is transmitted into the wall, leading to irate spouses or neighbours or both. Second, the headstock bearings wear out quickly. I would recommend bolting a lathe to a well weighted bench of its own.

The NU Tool lathe (and probably most of its aliases) is an adequate tool, but it is not a strong lathe, and to buy one does nothing to help the balance of payments or the lifestyles of the people who make them.

That said, I am very satisfied with it and feel I have transformed a cheap lathe into a much better one — without too much expense. ∎

A bowl of fruit turned on the modified lathe.

Assembled wheel.

Some of Andy's goblets.

Turned box on pedestal.

Miniature table, bottle and goblet, measured against a £1 coin.

Involuted turning, or inside out turning as it is sometimes called, can be used to make interesting shapes, as Peter Douglas reports.

ABOUT TURN!

Rubber bands hold the four squared parts together for the end pieces to be glued in place.

I think I may have re-invented the wheel when it comes to involuted turning. For my technique is different from the usual type of involuted work.

The latter consists of turning four pieces of square section wood as one piece, parting the pieces and turning each through 180DEG, before re-assembling and again turning as one unit.

I discovered that this technique could be varied by using two square pieces of wood or two rectangular ones – even three rhomboidal ones.

But my real breakthrough came when I turned four square pieces and rotated them through 90DEG (rather than 180DEG), with one or two further 90DEG steps, turning between each one.

This produces two solid ends connected by four 'legs', each with three or four sides or faces. You can turn a variety of shapes, depending upon the profile of each cut.

To make one of these shapes, take four square section pieces of wood. They must all be the same size as each other, but there's no limit to this size (other than lathe capacity).

The pieces for this project are about 32mm, 1¼" square x 200mm, 8" long. I fasten them together with rubber bands. An old inner tube is good for this.

If necessary, I present the ends to a sanding disc to get a flat surface. To each end, I glue a plate about 13mm, ½" thick made from scrapwood. The parts could

Arrows marked on the end show the original orientation.

The parts are dismantled, rotated 90DEG and re-assembled into a block for more turning.

After the second, more elaborate turning, arrows are re-marked when the end piece has been sawn off.

be glued using paper joints, but I prefer my method.

This unit is then centred in the lathe and a shape cut into it. Any shape will do, but I'm leaving about 25mm, 1" uncut at each end. At this stage I'll use a simple, concave curve.

After sanding and finishing the cut surface, I remove the unit from the lathe and dismantle it. To do this, I simply cut off the end plates. They can be used over and over again.

Each time I cut off the first plate, I mark the ends of the four pieces with arrows. This helps to avoid errors and makes it easier for me to describe what comes next.

I now turn my dismantled parts through 90DEG. The arrows look like those shown in the middle photo above, and I again fasten the pieces with elastic bands. The 25mm, 1" lengths of uncut material I suggested earlier, give enough space to locate the bands with ease.

The unit is now ready to have the end plates glued on again. I now repeat the

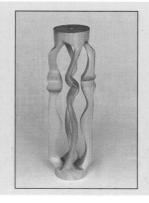

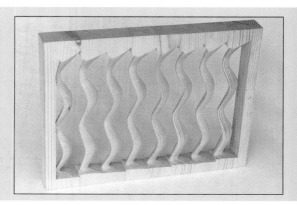

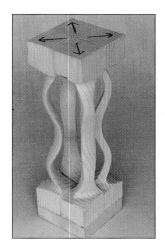

The components are rotated again then put back together for re-turning.

The assembly after the third cut, with the new arrows in place.

Rotated and banded, ready for the fourth time on the lathe

After four turning operations there are still more choices in assembling the components for the finished item. You could have radial symmetry ...

... all the parts facing the same way, or ...

whole process, only this time I'll be more adventurous and cut a more complex shape – a kind of wave.

New arrows are marked, as the original ones have been lost. With the pieces re-assembled, I turn them through 180DEG and make the next cut follow the shape of the last one, about 6mm ¼" from it.

This is easier than you might think, as when the wood is spinning, a 'shadow' of the previous cuts appears.

I could stop now, re-assemble the pieces as in the following photo, glue them together without end plates and use a fourth cut only to shape the ends. This would in itself make an interesting shape.

But I prefer to re-assemble the pieces with the end plates and make a fourth cut, following the outline of cut No. 1. When dismantled, I have four pieces which can be assembled in several different ways, some of which are shown right.

The arrows should make this clear. Where none are visible, the parts have been turned 'end for end'.

This technique can be used for simply decorative items (see below), for more practical things, such as candlesticks and lamp stands, or lanterns made from two or three identical sets of four pieces.

For something even more different, two or more identical sets can be joined in flat sheets. Or you can use a bandsaw or tablesaw to produce cross-sectional shapes (triangles, rhombi, hexagons etc), giving you yet more variations.

And how about square material tapered from one end to the other. There are still plenty of ideas to be explored.

I've had lots of fun and interest in making these shapes, but I must confess that none has turned out exactly as I expected. To define a piece by drawing the outline of each cut is fairly simple. But to envisage how it will look before or after is extremely difficult. ■

... you could invert some of the parts.

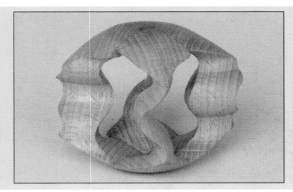

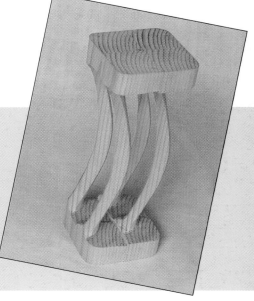

THE OUTER LIMITS

Ken Bradfield describes how to make flask-shaped vases using an offset turning jig.

Offset turning jig set-up. Two blocks are mounted at a time. Only the outsides can be turned. The drills in the end plate are locating pins, removed before turning starts.

I was pleased with the 'oval' vase I turned. But I realised the 'ovalness' was restricted because the centres had to be within the work's dimensions and wondered how to overcome this.

I worked out a way in which the centres can be positioned well beyond the piece of timber used. Instead of holding the wood directly between centres I support it in a jig. This allows me to have the centres a long way outside the normal limits.

I have two workpieces each placed at an equal distance from the lathe centres – up to 140mm, 5 ½in apart.

This allows me to cut a curved shape on only one side of each piece. To turn the other sides, each piece is rotated through 180° in the jig, then mounted back on the lathe.

You end up with a shape like that of a spirit flask, with two convex sides meeting at an apex.

After cutting the sides, I remove the work from the jig and each piece between centres.

The shoulder, where neck and body meet, could be cut straight across, but a curved shoulder is more pleasing.

I feel that this type of exaggerated off-centre turning is not very different from rough turning a piece of

Fig 1 Proportions of offset variations

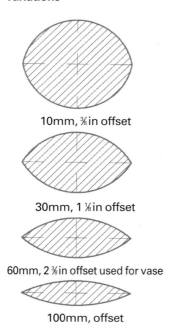

10mm, ⅜in offset

30mm, 1 ⅛in offset

60mm, 2 ⅜in offset used for vase

100mm, offset

Vase turned using an offset jig

One side turned. The toolrest is angled as a guide to the taper and waste is left at both ends to preserve the centre line.

branch wood. It's similar to any off-centre turning where there is intermittent cutting.

It is more dangerous than plain turning between centres, as the tip of the tool can 'drop' into the gap between workpieces. You have to be more careful at tool control.

To ensure the lathe is always balanced, the two offset workpieces must be at the same distance from the centre of rotation, and should start at about the same size and weight. You need not have the same variety of timber at each side, but they have to be about the same density.

If the workpieces start out balanced they will remain so,

▶

because the same weight is removed from each one with each cut.

For the jig, I used pieces of 9.5mm, ⅜in ply glued together to make 19mm, ¾in thick end pieces, but MDF or hardwood would do. I planed one edge straight for my face edge or datum.

On one face of each plate draw a line down the centre. Mark the middle of the line where the lathe centres will be located. Then mark the offset positions equidistant from the centres with a pair of compasses.

At the compass marks draw lines square to the centre line, then reset the compasses to 15mm, ¹⁹⁄₃₂in and strike marks for the screw holes.

Accurate marking out and drilling will make it easy to reposition the work – the screws will fit easily in both positions.

I temporarily hold the two parts of my jig together with panel pins and drill through both on a drill

Fig 2 Dimensions for a vase

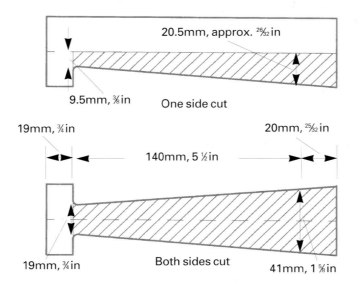

Both sides turned.

be restricted at the maximum offset, as it gets wider it will foul the lathe bed.

The jig is only rigid when the screws are tight in the blocks. The screws are into end-grain, which is weak, and digs may loosen their hold. Do check as you turn, for if the jig disintegrates it will throw the lot at you.

Before you switch on the lathe, spin the jig by hand to make sure it won't foul toolrest, banjo or anything else.

Rotating the blocks after the first offset turning operation is easier if you have a pivot.

This is why there is a 4 or 5mm, ⁵⁄₃₂ or ⁶⁄₃₂in hole between the screw holes for each block. I drill a shallow hole in the central position of each block, then use the drill or a pin as a pivot or locating pin.

The pivot holes are used to mount each piece between centres for turning the necks and will be turned off when the waste is parted off.

Making a vase

Before mounting blocks in the jig, mark a centre line down the sides and across the ends of each block. The screw holes for mounting them in the jig must be on this line, as this is the datum from which measurements are made.

Leave some wood each end roughly turned, so the lines remain. You can measure the minimum and maximum thickness of the taper on the unturned sections.

I use a roughing gouge for initial shaping. When I have a curve cut on the full width of the wood, I switch to scrapers. I use round nose scrapers and a Sorby replaceable tip scraper.

Fig 3 Jig for a two-sided vase at 60mm, 2 ⅜in offset

4mm, ⁵⁄₃₂in holes, drilled, countersunk No 8 screws

56mm, 2 ¹³⁄₆₄in
28mm, approx 1 ⅛in
15mm, ¹⁹⁄₃₂in
18mm, ²³⁄₃₂in
180mm, 7in
60mm, 2 ⅜in offset
2 off in ply, MDF or hardwood.

stand, to ensure accuracy.

The precision of the jig will be reflected in the regularity of the items turned on it.

On one plate I knock the four-prong drive centre into position to leave positive location marks. In the other, I drill a shallow countersink for the tail centre.

Use a wooden mallet on the end of the drive centre – if you put burrs on the end of the Morse taper it won't fit properly. Countersink the screw holes so the screw heads are set safely below the surface.

The maximum offset possible is dictated by the

centre height of the lathe and the degree of intrusion of the toolrest banjo. If you can tuck the toolrest banjo under the head or tailstock you'll be able to get maximum offset, but you may need an extra long toolrest to reach all of the workpiece.

The width of the work will

Hold handles firmly and keep the tool in positive contact with the toolrest and you should have no difficulty. Advance the tool carefully until it cuts, then traverse gently.

The vase's width is dictated by the thickness of the wood and the offset chosen (Fig 1). A 60mm, 2⅜in offset with a blank starting 45mm, 1¾in thick, gives proportions suitable for a small vase.

During offset turning, only the outside profiles of the workpieces are visible. When turning the first sides you cannot judge the finished thickness without stopping the lathe and measuring it from the centre line.

Same taper

To help get the same taper on both sides, when I have finished the first sides, I set the toolrest parallel to the taper and use it as a guide for the second sides. I don't move it until I have finished all the offset turning.

You can make items with curved sides, but you'll need to make a template so the curve is the same on both sides. The unturned sections at the ends are useful for locating the templates.

When I designed the vase I intended to drill a hole for a glass insert using a drill stand. I could have left a spigot on the base for holding in my Multistar chuck. Then I would have been able to use a drill in the tailstock.

As it was, I discovered that I should have left a spigot anyway, for I found it difficult to hold the tapered body in the drill vice. If held tightly in a vice, marks are left.

I also discovered that the hole for the insert shrinks as any residual moisture is lost.

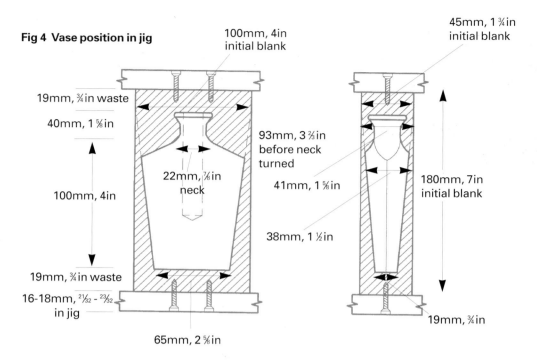

Fig 4 Vase position in jig

100mm, 4in initial blank

19mm, ¾in waste

40mm, 1⅝in

100mm, 4in

22mm, ⅞in neck

19mm, ¾in waste

16-18mm, ²¹⁄₃₂ - ²³⁄₃₂ in jig

65mm, 2⅝in

45mm, 1¾in initial blank

93mm, 3⅝in before neck turned

41mm, 1⅝in

38mm, 1½in

180mm, 7in initial blank

19mm, ¾in

Neck and base are turned between centres.

I've had this happen and a glass insert was gripped too tightly with a risk of it breaking. The only way to remove it was to wet the wood, causing it to expand.

I now drill my holes to a larger size than is recommended, allowing an extra 1 or 2mm, ³⁄₆₄ to ⁵⁄₆₄ in.

I've given the blank size as 100 x 45 x 180mm long and show the dimensions of the tapered sides and neck. Major changes in shape result if the thickness is increased and the neck proportions varied.

When the final turning is done between centres, I find it satisfying to make dramatic changes by simply changing the angle of the shoulder.

The angle here controls the curve at the top of the body and so is easy to vary.

It is important to allow enough thickness at the base for it to stand on. I find the minimum to be 16mm, ²¹⁄₃₂ in. In Fig 4 it's slightly bigger, at

19mm, ¾ in. It's not possible to sand the body with the lathe running, except around the neck.

Instead, I use an orbital sander and sanding discs in my electric drill. A 150mm, 6in low angle block plane removes any large protrusions.

I sometimes find it difficult to resist the temptation to remove the waste wood, in my hurry to see the final shape. I've learnt to resist this, because once gone it's difficult to re-mount the piece for any modifications ∎

As sanding with the lathe on is not possible, an orbital sander is used.

GETTING FASTER WITH FRICTION

Want to produce light pulls and other small items faster? Ian Wilkie tells you how in this article on his friction drive

Several years ago I was asked to make 50 plain beech light pulls. They were to be painted and sold at craft fairs. By the time I'd reached number 49 I thought there must be a quicker way of mounting and turning the blanks.

I went to the drawing board and my Unimat PC metal turning lathe to devise a simple, inexpensive, friction drive.

Trials

After some trials and experimentation I came up with a friction drive with three steps of 3, 6 and 10mm, ⅛, ¼ and ⅜in to match the different diameter of cord and knot-hole likely to be used.

I went on to develop the prototype to its full potential as other uses for this type of drive occurred to me.

Now the drive includes another step of 16mm, 21⁄32in, so that small bud vases can be turned. This will only work if a revolving centre is used in the tailstock.

There are several advantages to using the drive:

● Because it is a friction drive, the wood will stop rotating if the turner 'digs in' or makes a mistake. This makes it safer for the beginner.

● There are no sharp edges to catch unwary hands.

● As the pre-drilled blank is held between centres, the final turned item will have an absolutely true centre hole. In the case of a light pull or curtain pull this is particularly important, to ensure that the light pull hangs properly.

● The friction drive is relatively inexpensive.

I use the drive to turn a wide variety of items. I'll explain here how to use it to make light pulls, tool handles, chimney pots for a dolls' house, chessmen and a naval gun barrel.

A selection of light pulls.

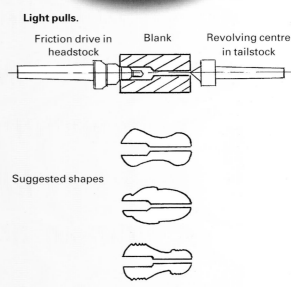

LIGHT PULLS

When I turn light pulls I use a 3mm, ⅛in cord hole and a 6mm, ¼in knot hole. But with curtain or blind pulls, which usually have a thicker cord, I drill a 6mm, ¼in cord hole and a 10mm, ⅜in knot hole.

I select a branch of about 40mm, 1⅝in diameter, or cut a 40 x 40mm square blank, 50 to 70mm, 2 - 2¾in long and mount the wood in a machine vice ready for drilling in the pillar drill.

The knot hole is drilled half way down into the blank using the depth stop on the pillar drill to control the depth of cut, and then the cord hole is drilled.

It helps to have extra-long HSS twist drills and these are available from Axminster Power tool Centre, Simbles and other good hardware shops.

The friction drive is placed in the headstock and a revolving centre in the tailstock. The blank is mounted on the friction drive and tailstock pressure provides the friction. With sharp tools it's surprising how little pressure is needed. The light pull is then turned to the desired shape, sanded and polished without remounting.

Light pulls.

Friction drive in headstock

Blank

Revolving centre in tailstock

Suggested shapes

▶

LIGHT PULLS

Because each step on the friction drive is sloped, with a groove at the bottom, a skew chisel point can cut right up to the edge of the hole, leaving a tidy finish.

The item can be removed, reversed and remounted to tidy up the other end. The drawing shows some suggested shapes, but it's fun to experiment with different designs and woods.

Naval gun barrel 1:18 scale.

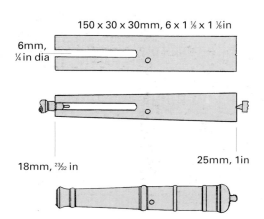

150 x 30 x 30mm, 6 x 1⅛ x 1⅛in

6mm, ¼in dia

18mm, ²³⁄₃₂ in

25mm, 1in

Cannon barrel mounted in the gun carriage.

NAVAL GUN BARREL

For the barrel for a 1:18 scale model of an 18th century naval gun, cut a blank 30mm, 1⅛in square and 150mm, 6in long and mark the centres at each end.

Choose a fine-grain wood such as Genero lemonwood or boxwood. Drill a 6mm, ¼in hole at one end to a depth of 70mm, 2¾in.

A gun barrel pivots on trunnions. On this model they are made with a dowel through the barrel. A hole for this should be drilled the same diameter as the bore.

Mount the blank between friction and tailcentres and turn to 25mm, 1in diameter.

Form a taper, 25mm at the tailstock end and 18mm, ²³⁄₃₂ in at the headstock end. Mark the position of the rings and fillets and, using the skew and the spindle gouge, shape the barrel.

Sand well and apply primer to the barrel before painting it matt black.

Shaping completed, and the cannon barrel painted.

TOOL HANDLES

The friction drive is particularly useful for making tool handles. Ferrules can be bought from Ashley Isles or cut from pipe.

A 30 x 30 x 190mm, 1⅛ x 1⅛ x 7½in blank of bocote was first centre marked at each end. One end was then drilled in the pillar drill with a 6mm, ¼in diameter bit to a 70mm, 2¾in deep hole. Special care was taken to ensure the hole was true.

A 17mm, 1⅟₁₆ in long brass ferrule with an 18mm, ²³⁄₃₂ in internal diameter was slipped over the friction drive and then the blank was also mounted on the drive.

The ferrule floats on the 16mm, ²¹⁄₃₂ in step and although it might rattle a little, it makes the task of turning the spigot to the correct diameter fairly easy. The handle does not need to be removed from the lathe until turning is finished.

After turning the blank to round and shaping the handle, the spigot was formed to give a good tight fit. Finally, the handle was sanded with Hermes RB 406 J-flex abrasive and polished with Record Speed-an-eese friction polish.

The blade can be glued into the handle with Araldite epoxy adhesive for added security.

Beech, European
Fagus sylvatica

Bocote
Cordia gerascanthus

Boxwood, European
Buxus sempervirens

Lemonwood, Genero
Calycophyllum multiflorum

Sycamore
Acer pseudoplatanus

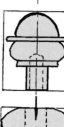

The 'humble curate' pawn.

Head

Blank 36 x 30 x 30mm, approx 1 ⅜ x 1 ⅛ x 1 ⅛ in, drilled 6mm, ¼ in dia

Body

Blank 50 x 30 x 30, 2 x 1 ⅛ x 1 ⅛ in, drilled 10mm, ⅜ in dia

CHESS PIECE

My chess pawn is a simple fellow, easy to make. He is based on a 19th century Austro/Hungarian chess set which had an ecclesiastical theme and represents a humble curate. I made him from sycamore and painted him with acrylic paints .

The body is made from a 30mm, 1 ⅛ in square blank 50mm, 2in long and drilled at one end with a 10mm, ⅜ in twist drill to a depth of 25mm, 1in.

The head is made from a 30mm square blank 36mm, about 1 ⅜ in long. One end is drilled with a 6mm, ¼ in diameter hole to a depth of 16mm, ²¹/₃₂ in.

The head is made separately from the body, as it is much easier to paint two separate parts.

The body blank is placed on the friction drive with tailstock support and turned to shape. The underside is formed slightly concave, so it will stand well on the chessboard. The long point of the skew is used for this.

The head blank is rounded on the friction drive with tailstock support. The 10mm, ⅜ in diameter 'neck' is easy to turn to size, using the 10mm step on the drive, which acts as a guide.

Truing off the base of the chessman body with the long point of the oval skew.

Turning the pawn's head's 10mm, ⅜ in spigot. Note the head is supported by the 6mm, ¼ in step and the 10mm acts as a guide for this diameter.

Fitting the head to the body after painting.

The remainder of the turning can be carried out with a 12mm, ½ in oval skew chisel.

Because the pieces were to be painted, the tailcentre dimple in the hat was filled with a wood filler and sanded smooth before painting.

Other pieces in the chess set are bigger, with grander head-wear to represent seniority.

▶

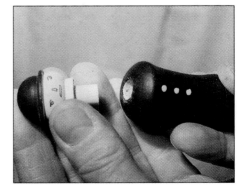

CHIMNEY POTS

I was asked to make a batch of 1:12 scale chimney pots 30mm, 1⅛in high with a maximum diameter of 20mm, ¾in. They were to be painted to represent terracotta.

Each pot was to have a 10mm, ⅜in centre hole 25mm, 1in . It is easier to pin and glue the pots to the top of the stacks if they are not drilled right through.

I cut 24mm, ¹⁵⁄₁₆ in square sycamore blanks 32mm, 1¼in long and drilled each one with a 10mm, ⅜in spur point drill.

Preparation of the blanks for repetitive turning is important – it must be accurate.

I mounted each blank in turn on the friction drive, supported by the revolving centre. After turning the blank to round with a roughing gouge, the chimney pot was shaped with a 13mm, ½in oval skew chisel.

I made a simple turning guide to aid repetitive turning and, with practise, made a large number of pots in a fairly short time.

Turning the chimney pots with the 13mm, ½in oval skew.

Some finished chimney pots.

Dolls' house chimney pot

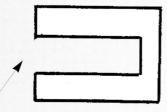

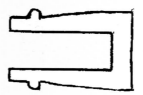

10mm, ⅜in dia   32 x 24 x 24mm, 1¼ x ¹⁵⁄₁₆ x ¹⁵⁄₁₆ in

The Ian Wilkie friction drive is made and sold by Axminster Power Tool Centre Ltd. It costs £9.50 plus p & p, for a No 1 or No 2 MT shank. Axminster Power Tool Centre, Chard Street, Axminster, Devon EX13 5DZ. Orders only, freephone 0800 371822. Fax: 01297 35242.

Conclusion

I've tried to show how versatile and safe the friction drive is. It can be used for many turning operations, providing the item to be turned has a 3, 6, 10 or 16mm hole and is to be turned between centres.

I have not included a design for a bud vase here, but it can be used successfully to turn them. They take a standard 16mm, ²¹⁄₃₂ in glass or plastic insert.

Turners asked to turn a number of these items for a craft fair or charity table, will find they can be made faster with this friction drive

The author

Ian Wilkie became a professional turner, specialising in miniature work, after leaving the Royal Air Force nine years ago. He originally became interested after making model ships.

He now tests new equipment and runs woodturning courses in Herefordshire. Ian is to be seen at many national woodworking shows and runs regular clinics at the Tewkesbury Saw Company.

Much of his time is spent writing about woodwork and woodturning and he is a regular contributor to specialist magazines.

THE BURNING QUESTION

Turners have always sought to embellish their work, and friction burning is one of the most effective ways of doing this, as Robert Wearing reports

Friction burning is one of the best ways to highlight a cut line, showing best on wilder grained woods, such as oak and elm. On lighter woods, such as sycamore, beech and holly, it can look like a thin ebony inlay.

Before plastic arrived, friction burning was often the only decoration on small boxes, cups, bowls, handles and knobs, all essentially household items.

Many of these Victorian products can be seen in craft and domestic museum collections.

The best wire for burning is the metalworkers' soft iron-binding wire, used to hold work together for soldering and brazing.

Several gauges are available. Florists' wire is similar and is sold in small rolls. Some is covered in paper, but this easily burns off. The roughness of this wire helps generate heat.

Polished copper wire is not so effective,

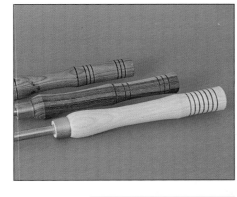

Turning tool handles can be easily identified by their burnt ring pattern.

Timbers

Oak, European
Quercus petraea &
Quercus robur

Elm, Dutch and English
Ulmus hollandica &
Ulmus procera

Sycamore
Acer pseudoplatanus

Beech, European
Fagus sylvatica

Holly
Ilex spp.

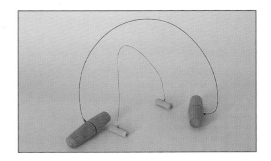

Attach a woodern toggle to each end of the wire, for safety.

while twisted wire, steel or copper, is likely to clog with carbon and burnt resin.

About 460mm, 18in is a good length to use. Twist a loop at each end and you'll have a good tool with which to injure, or even lose, a finger. Instead, turn a small wooden toggle for each end, then all will be safe.

When you are making more than two lines, mark them with dividers, on the toolrest. Point these steeply down, to avoid a dig-in. Iregularly-spaced lines are both obvious and ugly.

Vee groove

Increase the marking to a slight vee groove, using a parting tool on its side, not its edge. Again, point it down.

Remove the toolrest and pass the wire under the work, resting on the bed. Switch on, pull the wire taut, and raise it to engage in the vee groove.

Still taut, bring the hands towards each other, wrapping the wire halfway round the work. Smoke and smell will soon appear, but don't be put off.

Transfer to the other grooves and repeat. You needn't switch off. After burning, lightly sand the surface, but not the burnt groove, otherwise the crisp edges will be lost.

Clean out loose dirt from the groove by repeating the process with string of a suitable gauge.

After polishing, oiling and waxing, clean with string again, to give the groove a bright, jet finish.

Friction burning makes an admirable decoration for turning tool handles, the pattern making it easy to pick out the right tool from shavings. ∎

Burnt decoration camouflages the join on these mahogany boxes.

REST EASY

Canadian Douglas Angus describes the Last steady rest made by his friend Walter Last, which is said to make hollow turning easier

When turning the inside of a hollow form, an erratic rotation can develop if too much pressure is applied to the chisel. This can be overcome by using the Last steady rest, a lathe steady invented by Walter Last, of Winnipeg, Manitoba, Canada.

Walter's rest has been made from five lengths of 38 x 38 x 5mm, 1 ½ x 1 ½ x ³⁄₁₆ in, angle iron. The inside measurement is 178mm, 7in and the outside, 213mm, 8 ½ in, with the flange on the outer edge, away from the working area.

The base is one length of 6mm, ¼ in flat iron, 38mm wide by 267mm long, 1 ½ x 10 ½ in. Joints are welded to form a hexagon, with the right angle projections towards the chuck.

The flat iron base enables the

▶

The Last steady rest in position on the lathe bed, with arms supporting the workpiece for turning the interior.

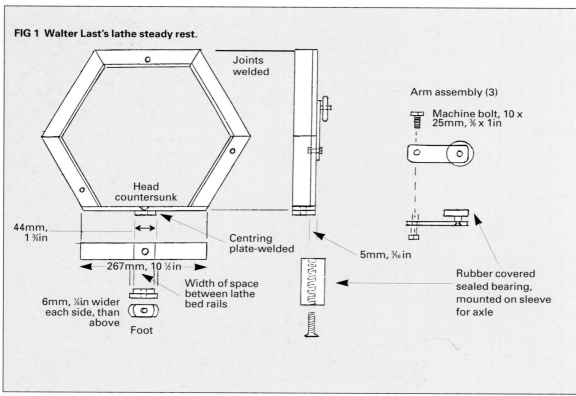

FIG 1 Walter Last's lathe steady rest.

Joints welded

Arm assembly (3)

Machine bolt, 10 x 25mm, ⅜ x 1in

Head countersunk

Centring plate-welded

44mm, 1 ¾in

5mm, ³⁄₁₆ in

267mm, 10 ½ in

Width of space between lathe bed rails

Rubber covered sealed bearing, mounted on sleeve for axle

6mm, ¼ in wider each side, than above

Foot

Arm assembly, showing the rubber-covered sealed bearing and mounting shaft.

accessory to be fitted to the lathe, as shown in the drawing. It will handle work of up to 280mm, 11in diameter.

About 38mm, 1½in from the end of the 178mm, 7in side, drill a 10mm, ⅜in hole through the vertical face to accept a machine bolt 25mm, 1in long, in the three positions shown.

Three arms, 38mm wide x 127mm, 1½ x 5in long, made from 6mm, ¼in plate, are drilled 20mm, ¾in in from each end. Use 10mm diameter, ⅜in holes.

One end accepts the mounting bolt, while the other is countersunk to permit mounting a 50mm, 2in rubber-covered sealed bearing. Use a 25mm, 1in long sleeve of exactly 12.7mm, ½in diameter and a flat head machine bolt through the arm in to the internally-threaded sleeve.

The sleeve's exterior provides the axle for the sealed bearing, which is why it must be the right size. Bolt the arms to the frame (bearings outward).

When mounted, they can be adjusted inwards to support the work being turned, and tightened to to maintain the support.

Attach the frame to the lathe bed by means of a piece of 6mm, ¼in plate, some 38mm, 1½in wide by the width of the space between the lathe bed rails.

Weld it to the underside of the bottom of the steady rest frame, in the centre, and drill through to accept a 10mm diameter, ⅜in flat head bolt, about 38mm, 1½in long. Use an Allen wrench head to insert it.

Locked in position

The plate centres the frame on the lathe bed and, when the foot beneath is in place and tightened, the whole thing is locked in position.

The foot consists of a piece of 6mm, ¼in plate, some 38mm, 1½in wide by the distance between the rails. This is welded to a similar-sized piece which projects 6mm, ¼in at each end to engage with the underside of the lathe bed rails when tightened (if your lathe has two square rails).

If your lathe has tubular rails, you will need to modify the mounting system. ∎

Sealed bearings

The rubber-covered sealed bearings referred to here have a tyre-like cover on the outer circumference.
They are a standard bearing insert of a steel cage pillow block and are rubber-covered to dampen vibrations.
Walter got his from an car reclaim company. UK readers can obtain them from Redhill Bearings, The White House, Brighton Road, Handcross, Redhill, Surrey (tel: 01444 400900).
He uses them for less critical work, where the slight play is not detrimental. But for more accurate work he prefers the more stable plain metal bearings. The main drawback in using the latter, he says, is the greater noise.
His procedure when using plain bearings is to mount the workpiece in the chuck (an expansion type which he also designed and machined) and turn the interior to a finished surface, including sanding and polishing.
He then removes the steady rest and turns the exterior, removing any track marks left by the metal bearings.

The author

Walter Last and A.J.Douglas Angus were former neighbours in Winnipeg, Manitoba.
Walter is the whizz in the workshop, while Douglas is more at home with the word processor, camera and drawing pen.
As a result, Walter does the designing and builds the prototype, while Douglas takes progress photos, makes drawings and does the write-ups to send to magazines.
Walter, who still lives in Winnipeg, grew up on a farm, and it was there that he learnt the art of innovation.
Doug Angus now lives in Richmond, British Columbia. He has developed a liking for woodworking that has led to him writing about it.

CUSTOM -BUILT

Terry Martin reports on how Brisbane turner Kevin Rosetta has customised his Vicmarc VL100 mini-lathe

For the woodturner with a new lathe in mind, there is a greater variety of machines available today than ever before. From compact mini-lathes to robust models suitable for large faceplate work, there is something for almost everyone.

But although a lathe might satisfy nearly all a turner's needs, something about it might not suit – and there's always some extra you want that never came with the lathe.

In cases like this, it's possible to modify your lathe. It doesn't always take special skills to make quite big improvements. The result can be a customised lathe which makes turning easier and adds to your pride in the work produced.

Of all the turners I know, no one takes more pride in his work and machinery than Kevin Rosetta. He works not far from my home in the city of Brisbane and when I have a technical problem I always go to him for a solution.

Kevin originally trained as wood machinist and has been a turner for 60 years. He has a wonderful mix of traditional skills and willingness to try anything new (Kevin's thread-cutting device was featured in *Woodturning* Issue 7). Kevin does a lot of demonstrating at craft shows and woodturning events, and for some time has wanted a robust, smaller lathe for this work. Recently he bought a locally made Vicmarc VL100 mini-lathe and I visited him to see the new machine.

Large

Solidly made from cast-iron, it has most of the features of a larger machine. But Kevin is a large man and he found the sheet-metal stand too low for him to comfortably work at.

He told me he was going to change it and I returned a week later to see the new stand. Nothing had prepared me for the changes he had made – it was as if he had made a whole new machine!

First, to raise the height Kevin had simply made a platform from scrap timber and had then attached the existing stand with turnbuckle-tensioned cable. It gave him the option of quick removal and meant that he didn't have to replace the original stand. (photo 1)

The VL100 has a between-centres capacity of 300mm, nearly 12in, which is fine for most small work. But Kevin decided he might want to turn that little bit extra and, in any case, it's always handy to have a slightly longer bed to park the tailstock out of the way.

He traced an outline of the end of the bed and then transferred it to a block of hardwood. After cutting out the shape on the bandsaw, he

Photo I Kevin's mini-lathe with the added stand.

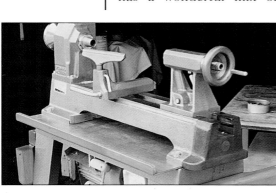

Photo 2 The bed extension, folding handles and tool tray with wooden tool protector.

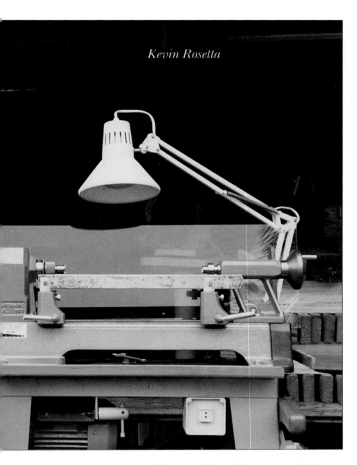

Kevin Rosetta

Photo 3 The sloped safety screen.

Photo 4 The turned sleeve on the engine mount.

refined it with a rasp and sandpaper and drilled a hole into one end.

He tapped a ⅜in thread into the end of the bed and bolted the extension on, then fitted a wooden plug into the hole to keep it all ship-shape.

Knowing that he would be loading and unloading the lathe from his van many times and moving it around at various venues, Kevin decided to make it easier for two people to hold on to.

Using the v-cuts in the end of the existing metal stand, he devised handles which slid up into the v and then were locked in place with wing nuts, again for easy removal if needed.

But the handles would obviously be in the way of a turner moving around on the business side of the lathe, so Kevin simply hinged them

to drop down out of the way when not in use.

As any demonstrator knows, there is never a convenient surface to put your tools on when you arrive at a turning venue. Kevin anticipated this by fitting a plywood shelf which simply slides into place between the bed and the stand and which extends right across the bed length.

Litttle extras

Then Kevin did something which is typical of the little extras which always delight me. He noticed that when he laid his tools on this shelf, there was a tendency for the cutting tips to bump against the bed of the lathe.

So he glued a small piece of wood in place to prevent damage to both the tools and

the lathe (photo 2).

Anyone who demonstrates a lot will know there is always concern about public liability. It is not only the big lathes with flying bits of wood which are dangerous. Children can get too close and put their fingers where they shouldn't. Also, shavings tend to fall out into walkways and need constant sweeping.

Kevin solved this with another simple, but well-planned, device. He attached

two arms to the carrying handles, again with wing nuts, and a slot cut in the arms allowed a piece of clear polycarbonate plastic to be inserted.

Again, he always thinks of those little extra touches – careful arrangement of the polycarbonate's slope means there are no reflections from the audience's side and they have an uninterrupted view

▶

Photo 5 The outboard end shelf.

of the work. The device is, again, easily removable (photo 3).

The lathe was provided with a wing nut to fasten the engine mount which is lifted to change pulleys. It worked well enough, but Kevin can't resist that extra touch: he replaced the wing nut with a bolt and turned a sleeve to fit over the end of it.

He then turned a tommy bar out of strong hardwood and inserted it through a hole drilled in the sleeve, capping it after insertion with a glued knob to prevent it sliding out.

Now he has easier access and operation every time he wants to change speeds, saving both time and fiddling around under the lathe (photo 4).

Kevin tried it all out and it worked well, but he couldn't help feeling it would be nice to have that little extra bit of shelf space.

On the outboard end he made another tray to slide over the safety screen mount. The addition of a single wing-bolt into the handle meant it was quite secure yet still easy to remove (photo 5).

Planet lamp

Because there is never enough light at turning venues, Kevin added a hole in the carrying handle at one end for the insertion of a planet lamp and then another hole in the other end so he could either move the lamp for certain work, or add another lamp if required.

This meant he would need an extra power outlet, so he attached a small powerboard to the stand.

For display of his finished small work he made up an extra shelf from an old metal stand and scrap ply.

Improvements

You might think that was enough, but no – Kevin never gives up on the improvements!

The standard toolrest was not long enough for the extended bed length, so he bought an extra tool rest holder and, using his metal lathe, he made up two slotted posts to fit into them.

He then cut a piece of 32 x 6 mm, 1¼in x ¼in metal stock to length and tapped through both the slotted posts and the bar for screws to hold it in place.

If he wants to slide the tailstock further in, he can simply remove the right-hand screw and the right-hand tool rest holder can slide to any position.

Because Kevin often uses an underhand grip when turning, he found that the bent handles on the tool rest holder (see photo 1) got in the way. So he replaced them with bolts and keeps the spanner held by a magnet on the shelf. When he is doing between-centres work, Kevin screws a protector on to the spindle thread in case a slip with the tool damages it. Kevin usually only turns lightweight work on this lathe, but he still uses an old trick which comes from working with bigger pieces on his other lathes. He inserts a Morse taper plug into the drive shaft, which effectively makes it into a solid bar.

He believes that when you have chucked or faceplate work on the lathe it makes the whole arrangement more solid. Frequently, when doing faceplate work, he puts a cork into the tailstock quill, which stops shavings getting into the Morse taper.

Understandably, Kevin is proud of his refinements. He gets such pleasure out of explaining them and seeing the delight on my face as each new idea is revealed.

When I told Kevin how much I admire the way he is always trying to think of new

Vicmarc lathes are available from:

Vicmarc Machinery, 52 Grice Street, Clontarf 4019, Queensland, Australia.
Tel: 0061 7 3284 3103.
Fax: 0061 7 3283 4656.

Vicmarc's UK agents: BriMarc Associates, 8 Ladbroke Park, Millers Road, Warwick, Warwickshire CV34 5AE.
Tel: 01926 493389.
Fax: 01926 491357.

improvements, he laughed. "Nothing's new!" he said. "One way or another it's all been done before."

None of these changes required special skills or equipment. The main tool he used was a band saw. All of the work was designed for quick assembly and required a minimum of drilling into the lathe or its stand.

Next time you are fumbling around with an uncomfortable set-up, do what Kevin does. Stop and look at how you are doing things and ask yourself if there is a better way? ■

Photo 6 The Morse taper plug and cork.

EUREKA!

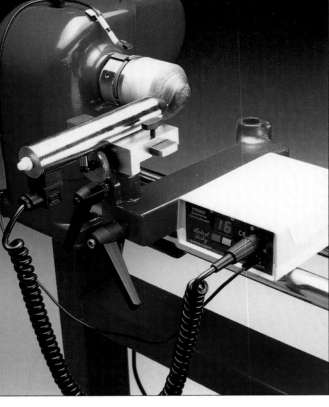

The RS3000 ornamental turning device set up on the lathe: the sensor on the headstock, the cutter assembly replacing the toolrest, and the Control Box.

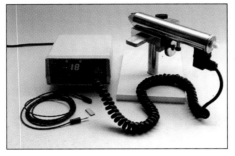

The RS3000 OT kit.

Martin Thompson-Oram describes how he spent four years developing a device to produce ornamental turned items on any lathe. The work is decorated in minutes while spinning at 500 RPM! The device is now being marketed by Robert Sorby, of Sheffield, as the RS3000

The RS3000 Ornamental Turning Device has been a long time in the making. How did it all start?

Turning is my living, not my hobby and, like everyone else, I wanted my work to be different. I had tried carving decoration by hand and the results were sometimes good, but the time involved made them difficult to sell.

I wanted to make something that would produce decoration without stop-ping the work, I needed it to be quick.

At the time I had not heard of ornamental turning and in spite of spending a great deal of time at antique fairs had never actually seen this kind of work. I didn't know how it was done or what it could look like.

The only thing that I had seen that could have been classed as ornamental turning was a Wedgwood black basalt creamer from the middle of the last century that I had been told was deco-rated with 'Engine Turning'.

I didn't know what that entailed, but it was probably something to do with pottery.

What I wanted was an easy way of indexing and cutting decoration, prefer-ably around curves while the work was turning.

On April 6, 1990, at about 2am, I had a flash of inspiration.

What about making a cutter that reci-procates in time with the revolving work? As the work passes the cutter, the latter moves in and cuts a piece out.

I thought, if I powered the cutter mechanism from the lathe itself, I should be able to synchronize the cutter, and if I had the cutter operating remotely, on the end of a cable, I could hold it where I wanted the decoration to be. Well, that was it. No sleep.

Impossible

As I wanted to produce pattern ele-ments that met at a point at their edges, I realized that the cutter would have to change direction instantly, which is phys-ically impossible.

So I had to figure out a cutting sequence that would allow the cutter time to change direction between one cut and the next.

That was the breakthrough I needed, though even so, the cutter would still have to be able to change direction many times per second.

Over the next several days I managed to make a mechanical device that proved without doubt that it was possible to make a row of cuts in a matter of seconds into the surface of a piece of work while it was revolving at 520 RPM, (the slowest speed at which my lathe will run), the shape of which could be predicted and-controlled.

I also found I could make clean precise cuts at any angle to the grain. There were disadvantages, however. The damn thing nearly made me deaf and the neighbours started to complain. I dare say James Watt had similar prob-lems.

During this early development I real-ized the process I was using demanded accuracy that was difficult to achieve. The cutter was accurate, but I wasn't accurate enough.

The positioning of the cutterbody in relation to the work needed to be exact in all directions, mainly because the cutter was not in contact with the work for most of the time, so if I moved the Cutterbody while it wasn't in contact, the next time it tried to make contact it dug a chunk out. Who said it was going to be easy?

A large piece of angle iron made a flat toolrest, and by giving the stem of this rest a collar I could ensure the cutter

approached the work at exactly the same height at all times.

By trial and error I discovered that the most effective height was level with centre.

About this time I started to get some attractive results, which was encouraging, though there were still many problems to overcome, the rake angle of the cutter being one.

As the cutter dives below the surface of the work at the beginning of a cut and is pulled out from below the surface at the end of a cut, the rake angle effectively changes.

At no time during a cut can the cutter work as a conventional turning tool with the bevel rubbing on the cut surface of the work, so the rake angle of the cutter had to be found by trial and error to give the best average result over a wide range of timbers.

By this time I was excited, partly by the ease and speed with which I could decorate work, and partly because I had

How the shape of the cuts alters for a given stroke length as the radius of the work decreases.

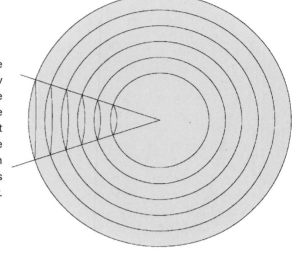

The depth that the cutter will dip below the surface of the work remains the same, so the cut becomes more curved as the length of the cut becomes shorter.

The offset of each row of cuts can be precisely controlled to give basket weave and spiral effects.

found out how ornamental turning had been done in the past.

I felt I had stumbled on something that could be of use to other people. I had certainly never seen anything that operated in the same way, so I continued to refine it.

I produced some good work with it, but quickly realised that if it was going to be useful to a lot of people, I wasn't in a position to manufacture it. I had to find someone who was. I presented the idea to Robert Sorby.

They were encouraging, perhaps quite excited, but had reservations.

I am the first to admit there were things wrong with it, a major one being how to fix it easily to any lathe. Obviously, if it couldn't be fitted to just about any lathe, nobody would be very interested.

However, spurred on by their reaction, after much thought and struggle I produced an electronic version of the device using the same principles, which

could be fitted to any lathe, and the RS3000 was born.

All that was fixed to the lathe now was a sensor and a magnet. Nothing needed to be modified, and more importantly anyone could use it. It also had some distinct advantages over the mechanical device, a major one being noise.

What we now have is an Electronically Controlled Self-Indexing Reciprocating Cutter, and it looks and operates like nothing you have ever seen before. There are two main parts to it, the Control Box, and the Cutterbody.

The Control Box contains a microprocessor that works out how fast the lathe is running, and where the workpiece is at any given moment. It also monitors the lathe speed continuously and adjusts the timing of the cutter impulses if the speed changes.

It has a memory containing the information that it needs to position the cutter at the spacings that you have chosen. It also allows you to turn off the lathe to see how the decoration is developing, then to re-start the lathe and continue cutting at those same positions.

The Control Box is operated by two push switches below the display panel. The left-hand one changes the function, i.e. pattern, number of cuts and offset, while the right-hand changes the value of the chosen function.

There are six basic patterns of cut to

choose from in the memory, which cause cuts to be made at 6, 8, 12, 16, 18, and 24 positions around the workpiece, evenly spaced.

All these patterns can be revolved relative to each other using the offset function, so that cuts in adjacent rows can be differently aligned.

This gives the opportunity to easily create spiralling patterns by offsetting adjacent rows of cuts.

This function rotates the positions of the cuts around the workpiece 2.5 degrees at a time. There comes a time when the cuts are offset by one full cut, so the number of possible offsets varies according to how many cuts are being made.

The switches can also turn the cutter off without losing the pattern that has been selected.

There is not much to operating it really, most of the thinking is done by the microprocessor. All you have to do is select a pattern of cut positions using the buttons on the front. The display on the Control Box tells you what has been selected, leaving you free to be creative, operating the Cutterbody.

The Cutterbody contains the mechanism which drives a small cutter backwards and forwards by a controlled amount, many times per second. (The number of times per second that it moves depends on how fast the lathe is running, and what pattern of cuts has been selected.)

On the back of the Cutterbody is the stroke control. This controls the length of the cutter stroke, which governs the depth that the cutter will dip below the surface of the workpiece before the cuts meet at their ends.

The rest of the equipment that comes with the machine has been designed to assist the operator to position the cutter accurately, and to control the rate at which the cutter is fed into the work.

Because the cutter will cut to the same depth below surface with any given stroke length and cut selection, the cuts are more sharply curved on smaller diameters.

The stroke control allows you to adjust the length of the stroke to suit the diam-

How the cutting angle (x) changes relative to the cut during the cutting action.

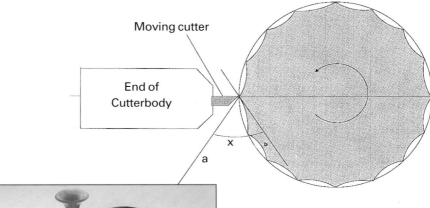

The RS3000 can handle a range of sizes, down to button sized work.

eter of the work, to cut shallower patterns, or to fade patterns out.

During the development I discovered I could easily decorate items as small as 6mm, ¼" in diameter, or even less on end grain.

In short, the machine is completely controllable, its operating procedures combining traditional hand skills with the simple use of modern electronics.

Once the best site for the sensor has been found, and the guide support stem fitted to the guide support, using it couldn't be simpler.

The sensor needs to be mounted somewhere stable, where the magnet will pass within about 3mm, 1⅛" of it. The magnet needs to be fixed to the headstock shaft, the chuck, or the workpiece – anywhere on the lathe that is spinning at the same speed as the work. The Cutterbody guide assembly fits in the place of the standard toolrest.

The cutter cuts precisely at the indexed positions. By changing the cutter shape and the depth of the cuts below the surface, offsetting adjacent rows of cuts and altering the number of cuts in the rows, the operator can cut an enor-

mous range of decoration onto rotating work using an ordinary lathe, in a fraction of the time that traditional methods would have taken.

The decoration can be limited to a simple border, or the whole of the surface of an item may be decorated to give a textured effect.

To produce this manner of decoration in the past was a lengthy process requiring a large amount of costly equipment which is generally not available today.

The work needed to be accurately positioned and stationary to enable each cut to be made individually by a separately powered cutter.

Some patterns of decoration that are possible with the RS3000 are unique. ■

The author

Martin Thompson-Oram was born in 1951 and started woodturning in 1979 to help in the restoration of antiques.
He builds most of his own machinery and set up his own business as a full time woodturner and cabinet maker in 1989.
He has exhibited his work at craft exhibitions, and has won some competitions.

INDEX

GMC Publications

BOOKS

WOODWORKING

40 More Woodworking Plans & Projects	*GMC Publications*	Making Chairs and Tables	*GMC Publications*
Bird Boxes and Feeders for the Garden	*Dave Mackenzie*	Making Fine Furniture	*Tom Darby*
Complete Woodfinishing	*Ian Hosker*	Making Little Boxes from Wood	*John Bennett*
Electric Woodwork	*Jeremy Broun*	Making Shaker Furniture	*Barry Jackson*
Furniture Projects	*Rod Wales*	Pine Furniture Projects for the Home	*Dave Mackenzie*
Furniture Restoration (Practical Crafts)	*Kevin Jan Bonner*	Sharpening Pocket Reference Book	*Jim Kingshott*
Furniture Restoration and Repair for Beginners	*Kevin Jan Bonner*	Sharpening: The Complete Guide	*Jim Kingshott*
Green Woodwork	*Mike Abbott*	Woodfinishing Handbook (Practical Crafts)	*Ian Hosker*
The Incredible Router	*Jeremy Broun*	Woodworking Plans and Projects	*GMC Publications*
Making & Modifying Woodworking Tools	*Jim Kingshott*	The Workshop	*Jim Kingshott*

WOODTURNING

Adventures in Woodturning	*David Springett*	Practical Tips for Turners & Carvers	*GMC Publications*
Bert Marsh: Woodturner	*Bert Marsh*	Practical Tips for Woodturners	*GMC Publications*
Bill Jones' Notes from the Turning Shop	*Bill Jones*	Spindle Turning	*GMC Publications*
Bill Jones' Further Notes from the Turning Shop	*Bill Jones*	Turning Miniatures in Wood	*John Sainsbury*
Colouring Techniques for Woodturners	*Jan Sanders*	Turning Wooden Toys	*Terry Lawrence*
Decorative Techniques for Woodturners	*Hilary Bowen*	Understanding Woodturning	*Ann & Bob Phillips*
Essential Tips for Woodturners	*GMC Publications*	Useful Techniques for Woodturners	*GMC Publications*
Faceplate Turning	*GMC Publications*	Useful Woodturning Projects	*GMC Publications*
Fun at the Lathe	*R.C. Bell*	Woodturning Jewellery	*Hilary Bowen*
Illustrated Woodturning Techniques	*John Hunnex*	Woodturning Masterclass	*Tony Boase*
Intermediate Woodturning Projects	*GMC Publications*	Woodturning Techniques	*GMC Publications*
Keith Rowley's Woodturning Projects	*Keith Rowley*	Woodturning Test Reports	*GMC Publications*
Make Money from Woodturning	*Ann & Bob Phillips*	Woodturning Wizardry	*David Springett*
Multi-Centre Woodturning	*Ray Hopper*	Woodturning: A Foundation Course	*Keith Rowley*
Pleasure and Profit from Woodturning	*Reg Sherwin*	Woodturning: A Source Book of Shapes	*John Hunnex*

WOODCARVING

The Art of the Woodcarver	*GMC Publications*	Useful Techniques for Woodcarvers	*GMC Publications*
Carving Birds & Beasts	*GMC Publications*	Wildfowl Carving - Volume 1	*Jim Pearce*
Carving on Turning	*Chris Pye*	Wildfowl Carving - Volume 2	*Jim Pearce*
Carving Realistic Birds	*David Tippey*	The Woodcarvers	*GMC Publications*
Decorative Woodcarving	*Jeremy Williams*	Woodcarving for Beginners	*GMC Publications*
Essential Tips for Woodcarvers	*GMC Publications*	Woodcarving Test Reports	*GMC Publications*
Essential Woodcarving Techniques	*Dick Onians*	Woodcarving Tools, Materials & Equipment	*Chris Pye*
Lettercarving in Wood: A Practical Course	*Chris Pye*	Woodcarving: A Complete Course	*Ron Butterfield*
Practical Tips for Turners & Carvers	*GMC Publications*	Woodcarving: A Foundation Course	*Zoë Gertner*
Understanding Woodcarving	*GMC Publications*		

UPHOLSTERY

Seat Weaving (Practical Crafts)	*Ricky Holdstock*	Upholstery Techniques & Projects	*David James*
Upholsterer's Pocket Reference Book	*David James*	Upholstery: A Complete Course	*David James*
Upholstery Restoration	*David James*		

TOYMAKING

Designing & Making Wooden Toys	*Terry Kelly*	Making Character Bears	*Valerie Tyler*
Fun to Make Wooden Toys & Games	*Jeff & Jennie Loader*	Making Wooden Toys & Games	*Jeff & Jennie Loader*
Making Board, Peg & Dice Games	*Jeff & Jennie Loader*	Restoring Rocking Horses	*Clive Green & Anthony Dew*

DOLLS' HOUSES

Architecture for Dolls' Houses	*Joyce Percival*	Making Miniature Oriental Rugs & Carpets	*Meik & Ian McNaughton*
Beginners' Guide to the Dolls' House Hobby	*Jean Nisbett*	Making Period Dolls' House Accessories	*Andrea Barham*
The Complete Dolls' House Book	*Jean Nisbett*	Making Period Dolls' House Furniture	*Derek & Sheila Rowbottom*
Dolls' House Bathrooms: Lots of Little Loos	*Patricia King*	Making Tudor Dolls' Houses	*Derek Rowbottom*
Easy to Make Dolls' House Accessories	*Andrea Barham*	Making Unusual Miniatures	*Graham Spalding*
Make Your Own Dolls' House Furniture	*Maurice Harper*	Making Victorian Dolls' House Furniture	*Patricia King*
Making Dolls' House Furniture	*Patricia King*	Miniature Needlepoint Carpets	*Janet Granger*
Making Georgian Dolls' Houses	*Derek Rowbottom*	The Secrets of the Dolls' House Makers	*Jean Nisbett*

CRAFTS

Celtic Knotwork Designs	*Sheila Sturrock*	Embroidery Tips & Hints	*Harold Hayes*
Collage from Seeds, Leaves and Flowers	*Joan Carver*	Making Greetings Cards for Beginners	*Pat Sutherland*
Complete Pyrography	*Stephen Poole*	Making Knitwear Fit	*Pat Ashforth & Steve Plummer*
Creating Knitwear Designs	*Pat Ashforth & Steve Plummer*	Pyrography Handbook (Practical Crafts)	*Stephen Poole*
Cross Stitch Kitchen Projects	*Janet Granger*	Tassel Making for Beginners	*Enid Taylor*
Cross Stitch on Colour	*Sheena Rogers*	Tatting Collage	*Lindsay Rogers*

THE HOME

Home Ownership: Buying and Maintaining	*Nicholas Snelling*	Security for the Householder: Fitting Locks and Other Devices	*E. Phillips*

VIDEOS

Drop-in and Pinstuffed Seats	*David James*	Twists and Advanced Turning	*Dennis White*
Stuffover Upholstery	*David James*	Sharpening the Professional Way	*Jim Kingshott*
Elliptical Turning	*David Springett*	Sharpening Turning & Carving Tools	*Jim Kingshott*
Woodturning Wizardry	*David Springett*	Bowl Turning	*John Jordan*
Turning Between Centres: The Basics	*Dennis White*	Hollow Turning	*John Jordan*
Turning Bowls	*Dennis White*	Woodturning: A Foundation Course	*Keith Rowley*
Boxes, Goblets and Screw Threads	*Dennis White*	Carving a Figure: The Female Form	*Ray Gonzalez*
Novelties and Projects	*Dennis White*	The Router: A Beginner's Guide	*Alan Goodsell*
Classic Profiles	*Dennis White*	The Scroll Saw: A Beginner's Guide	*John Burke*

MAGAZINES

WOODTURNING ◆ WOODCARVING ◆ TOYMAKING
FURNITURE & CABINETMAKING ◆ BUSINESSMATTERS
CREATIVE IDEAS FOR THE HOME ◆ THE ROUTER

◆

The above represents a full list of all titles currently published or scheduled to be published. All are available direct from the Publishers or through bookshops, newsagents and specialist retailers. To place an order, or to obtain a complete catalogue, contact:

GMC Publications,
166 High Street, Lewes, East Sussex BN7 1XU United Kingdom
Tel: 01273 488005 Fax: 01273 478606

Orders by credit card are accepted